From the High Plains

Books by John Fischer

WHY THEY BEHAVE LIKE RUSSIANS
MASTER PLAN: U.S.A.
THE STUPIDITY PROBLEM AND OTHER HARASSMENTS
VITAL SIGNS, U.S.A.
FROM THE HIGH PLAINS

Drawings by Paul Laune

From the High Plains

John Fischer

HARPER & ROW, PUBLISHERS
NEW YORK, HAGERSTOWN, SAN FRANCISCO, LONDON

Portions of this work originally appeared in *Harper's Magazine*.

FIRST EDITION

Designed by Gloria Adelson

Library of Congress Cataloging in Publication Data

Fischer, John, date
　From the high plains.
　　1. Texas—History—Miscellanea. 2. Oklahoma —History—Miscellanea. 3. Great Plains—History —Miscellanea. I. Title.
F386.F57 1978　　976.4'8　　78-437
ISBN 0-06-011269-7

78 79 80 81 82 10 9 8 7 6 5 4 3 2 1

For Meg and Sarah and Nick and Charley

Contents

Prologue   1

ONE
Mr. Baxter and the Butchering   5

TWO
Why the High Plains Were Settled So Late   17

THREE
Reluctant Pioneer   31

FOUR
Colonel Goodnight and the British Connection   45

FIVE
Legends: Here Today and Gone Today, Too   59

SIX
The Misleading History of Old Tascosa   71

SEVEN
Barbed Wire and the Art of Stringing It   91

EIGHT
Geronimo's Magic Blanket   107

NINE
The Sayings   123

TEN
Growing Up on the Salt Fork   137

ELEVEN
Oil   153

TWELVE
Unsettled Country   169

Acknowledgments   180

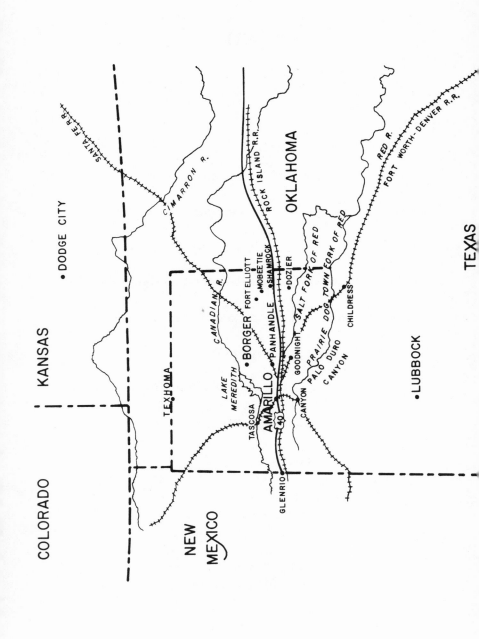

Prologue

By a quirk of geography, I was born in the last part of the United States to be settled. This is the High Plains, a plateau, about half a mile above sea level, that lies in the heart of a much larger grassland area, the Great Plains. The latter stretches from the Rocky Mountains to the middle of the Mississippi Valley, north beyond the Canadian border, and south into Mexico. The High Plains lie mostly in the Panhandles of Texas and Oklahoma, straggling at the edges into neighboring states. For peculiar reasons, to be noted a little later, the flood of settlement had streamed past this country, both to the north and to the south, leaving it to the buffalo and the Indians who preyed upon them, long after south Texas, the northern Plains, and even the West Coast had a considerable white population.

My parents were among the early settlers of the High Plains, and some of their friends were, in fact, the earliest. So it happened that I got to know Col. Charles Goodnight, who started the first ranch there after half a lifetime of fighting against the Comanches and Apaches. My grandfather Fischer was a friend of Geronimo, the last of the Indian war chiefs to contest white settlement of the High Plains; if I had been born eighteen months earlier, I might very well have been introduced to the old warrior during one of my grandfather's frequent visits to Geronimo's last home at Fort Sill, Oklahoma. For the Fischer family had homesteaded 160 acres between the fort and the neighboring village of Apache, a farm that my brother and I eventually inherited. My grandfather Caperton's family homesteaded the first ranch at Dozier, Texas, on the Salt Fork of the Red River, and my mother grew up there in a sod shanty, known locally as a "dugout" because it was half underground. Nearly all my male relatives were cowboys or, in later life, ranchers or farmers.

I am a survivor, then, of a generation that saw the last of the Old West slide around the corner of history. It was not a numerous generation, because the High Plains of my boyhood were sparsely peopled—much of the area still is—and few of my contemporaries ever bothered to write about that time and place. This I regret, because I could use some witnesses to back me up. Many of my friends think they already know all about the Old West from television and John Wayne movies. Although they may realize that TV commercials are mostly lies, they still believe that the TV version of Western history is true, or at least plausible. I have made scant headway in persuading them that what really happened was more interesting, though less dramatic and far less bloody.

So this account is an attempt to document some remnant of the last frontier as it was remembered by eyeball witnesses. What my kinfolk and other old-timers told me was, I think, mostly true; whenever possible I have tried to check their stories against written records. But some of their yarns were, I suspect, legend or folklore. A few of these I have included anyway, because they reflect so accurately the character of the tellers. On the other hand, what I took for tall tales were occasionally, as I discovered later, the literal truth. So it was with some of Mr. Baxter's.

ONE

Mr. Baxter and the Butchering

The summer I was ten years old, Mr. Robert L. Baxter gave me my first paid job as a cowboy. I had ridden horses since I was about four, and had worked with cattle enough to regard them as stupid, unreliable, and often hysterical beasts. But nobody ever dreamed of paying for that or for my other household chores, including chopping firewood, feeding chickens, churning butter, and cleaning kerosene lamps. Mr. Baxter's hiring me was mostly nepotism. He was my uncle, and I was living that summer with his family in their rambling frame house on the southern edge of Shamrock, Texas. He paid me and my cousin Robert, of the same age, five dollars a month and found. "Found," a common word then but no longer much used, meant room, board, and working equipment, such as a horse, saddle, and rope.

Our salary was generous for the work we did. It had no resemblance to anything you may have seen in a Western film.

Most days we herded a couple of dozen steers from the Baxter pasture to my Uncle Claude Caperton's pasture, about ten miles away, where the grass was a little better. Unlike TV cowboys, who always seem to ride at a high lope, we just shambled across the prairie, for two reasons: the slower you move cattle, the less weight they sweat off; and our horses could seldom be kicked into anything faster than a walk.

Mine was an elderly white mare with a rare talent: she could sleep while walking. Robert's was an equally lazy roan gelding named Rosy. (All of Robert's animals were named Rosy, including his dog, two cats, and a banty rooster. His theory was that when he hollered "Rosy!" they would all assemble, like a squad of well-drilled infantry. I never saw this happen.) Our work was not romantic; it was merely hot, dusty, and dull. (Anybody who thinks his present job is a bore should try contemplating the rear elevation of a steer for a few days.) When the steers reached the Caperton place we watered them at a galvanized iron tank filled by a windmill, and turned them into the fenced pasture. We were then free to take a dip in the tank ourselves—it was, like most ranch tanks, about three feet deep and a dozen across—and eat our lunch in the shade of the Caperton house. This was not only living quarters, originally built by my grandfather, but also post office and country store. The Capertons were hereditary postmasters of Dozier, and selling a few groceries was no extra trouble. Sometimes Uncle Claude would give us a cream soda pop to go with the sandwiches we brought in sugar sacks tied behind our saddles. He was fat, bald, and—like most Caperton men of that generation—both charming and lazy.

After lunch we usually practiced roping for a while, on the Caperton calves or a post in the corral. I never was any good at it. Now and then I would catch a calf with a hoolihan throw, which begins with a large loop trailing on the ground to your right. At the proper moment you flip it overhand to your front and left, in hopes that it will pass over the head and body of a running calf and tighten around his hind hocks. Often my rope would tighten around his ribs, which resulted in his throwing me rather than me him. Robert was much better than I was at roping and most other ranch work, even though he was smaller. He had been a premature baby—his mother, my Aunt Myrtle, liked to tell how his first crib was a shoe box stuffed with cotton—but to everybody's surprise he survived and grew up tough and wiry. In 1932 he inherited the Baxter ranch and worked it until a few years ago, when he died after a horse fell on him.

In midafternoon we started home, making a little better time because we had no cattle with us and because the horses, knowing they would be fed when we got there, could sometimes be coaxed into a canter. We got fed, too, after we had tended to the horses, hung up our saddles, and taken care of whatever chores Aunt Myrtle had in mind for us. And then, sometimes, as the sun dipped out of sight and the fireflies came out, Robert and I could persuade Mr. Baxter to tell us a story

He always sat in a rocking chair on the front porch, wearing the Boss of the Plains brand Stetson hat that he put on when he got out of bed and took off only when he ate a meal indoors. Robert and I planned to get hats just like it when we grew up, and high-heeled boots like his, too. Meanwhile we made do with straw hats and sneakers—though the rest of our clothes, blue jeans and blue huck shirts, were the same as his. Mr. Baxter talked little, and reluctantly, so it wasn't easy to coax him into a story. As I remember it, an evening conversation might go about like this:

"Did you ever shoot any Indians, Mr. Baxter?" (Everybody called him that, including his wife and usually Robert, although "Dad" was tolerated from his children.)

"Nope."

"Did you ever shoot any outlaws?"

"Nope. Never had any call to shoot anybody."

"Well, did anything exciting ever happen to you when you were a cowboy?"

"Not that I can recall. Unless you could call that trouble with the old mossyhorns exciting."

"What trouble?"

"Well, when I was a youngster, maybe sixteen or seventeen, I got a job hunting wild cattle down in east Texas. That country is a lot different from ours. It gets plenty of rain, so that thickets of heavy brush grow up along all the creeks and bosques—mostly shinnery oak and mesquite, chapparal, and prickley pear. None of the land was fenced in those days, and even the best cow hands couldn't keep an eye on a big herd day and night. So a good many cattle, especially the young bulls, slipped away and hid in the brush. After they had been there a few weeks they got so wild it was impossible to drive them out into the open range, even if you could find them.

"Some of the stockmen made a standing offer of five dollars a head for any of those wild ones that a cowboy could catch and deliver back to the herd. They didn't have many takers. Since my friend Bud Withers and I didn't have steady jobs then, we decided we might as well see what we could do in the thickets.

"At first we didn't have any luck at all. The cows were all longhorns then, not the gentle half-Hereford crosses that we are raising here, and they were mighty mean. They could bust their way through brush faster than a horse, and if you got too close they were sure to hook you. Besides, the eight-inch thorns on the mesquite bushes could tear up horses and riders pretty bad. They could even tear through leather chaps. That's why we took to wearing fur chaps, made of bear skin. They gave better protection.

"Finally Bud and I discovered that if we worked close together, one of us slipping up on one side of a wild bull and one on the other, one of us could get a rope on him pretty often. But that didn't solve our problem. Those old bulls were too heavy and too mean to drag out of the thicket, even if you got two ropes around their neck. They would strangle first.

"Then we got a tip from an old-timer. He told us to get some needles and linen thread, which we found at the nearest store. From then on, when we got our ropes on a wild one, we would throw him and hogtie him, front legs and back. Then Bud would sit on his head while I sewed up his eyelids. That worked like a charm. Once he couldn't see, even the orneriest bull would turn plumb bewildered and docile. It was easy to lead him to the nearest herd or corral. By the time the thread rotted, he was usually pretty well tamed. And in any case, Bud and I had collected five dollars.

"We learned another trick in East Texas. If a yearling bull or steer got caught two or three times trying to sneak away from the herd, the old hands knew a way to discourage him. They would throw and tie him, and then fix the tassle of hair at the end of his tail. First they would comb it out, nice and smooth, and divide it down the middle. Then they would make two braids and knot the ends, so they had a sort of hair loop. When you slipped this into the cleft of one of the critter's hind hoofs, he was right well hobbled. He couldn't get that foot down to the ground, so he had to bob around on three legs. And if he tried to kick, he pulled his own tail and probably got a pain in the hoof cleft at the same time.

"Of course the braids worked loose after a few days, but by that time the steer was some domesticated. Leastwise, he wasn't so likely to head for the brush for quite a while."

"Why did you call the wild ones 'mossyhorns,' Mr. Baxter?"

"Because they had moss on their horns, of course. Anyhow, the older ones. After they had lived in those swamps and wet thickets for a year or two, they grew moss, like most everything else around.

"I expect a man would, too, if he lived in east Texas long

enough. Before I was twenty I went north, helping trail a herd to Dodge City, and never went back. Like Shanghai Pierce said, that East Texas country ain't fit for raising anything except walruses."

I didn't believe any of this. I thought Mr. Baxter had just made up a tall story to amuse us kids. But thirty years later both Frank Dobie and Walter Prescott Webb told me that eyelid sewing was a common practice in the early days of brush country ranching. Those two ought to know; they were the best historians Texas has yet produced.*

I still don't know whether to believe the braided tassel story. No cow that I've ever inspected had tail hair long enough to make a good loop. But maybe the longhorns grew more hair, just as they grew more horn; they sure didn't grow much beef.

Mr. Baxter did all right after he moved to the High Plains. He got there about 1886, just as the country was opening up for settlement, and had no trouble getting work with the Rocking Chair, Mill Iron, and other early ranch outfits. He soon became foreman of the Mill Iron† and evidently was a popular one, because when he retired the hands who worked under him chipped in money to buy him a fancy saddle, hand tooled, with a silver horn and mountings. It was his proudest possession, and so far as I know he never used it; it stayed on a sawhorse in the attic.

While he was still a cow hand, Mr. Baxter homesteaded a section—640 acres—and began to build up a herd of his own. Some cows he bought. Others were unbranded calves that had somehow got separated from their mothers, so-called mavericks.‡ Perhaps some came from one or another of the British-

---

*See Dobie's *The Longhorns* (Boston: Little, Brown, 1941), p. 310.

†The Mill Iron brand looks like this ⊃⊂. Two pieces of metal shaped like that were often used to hold the shafts of some kinds of milling machinery. The Rocking Chair looked like this ⊃Ɫ.

‡The first ranchers in Texas didn't bother with brands. But when the range got so crowded that their herds began to get mixed up, they held a meeting

owned ranches, which were sometimes badly managed because
of absentee ownership and thus unpopular with the cowboys.
There is reason to believe that their calves got lost pretty often,
and not always by accident. More about these ranches later.
Anyhow, before he was middle-aged, Mr. Baxter was able to
quit being a hired man on horseback and to start ranching on
his own.

That summer he was sixty years old and seemed older, because he suffered from the usual occupational diseases—
rheumatism from many nights sleeping on wet ground, badly
set bones, a slipped disk or two, and hemorrhoids. Most of his
time he spent in his rocking chair, but there was one job he
always supervised himself: the monthly butchering. Robert and
I looked forward to it, because it was the closest thing to an adventure that came our way that summer.

On his orders we would cut out the fattest yearling we could
find, get a rope around his throat, and drag him to a heavy
cedar post set in the Baxter backyard. When we had the steer
snubbed up close to the post, Mr. Baxter would rouse himself
from the porch and hobble out to join us. He brought with him
a twelve-pound sledge hammer. Lifting this high above the
head of the now immobilized steer, he took careful aim and hit

and decided that branding would be the most practical solution. Each man
present announced what brand he planned to use—all except old Sam Maverick. He sat quietly in the back of the room until all the others had named their
brands. Then he said, "I guess I don't need one. Since all your cattle will be
marked, you will know that all the unbranded ones belong to me." They let
him get away with this for several years. So, at least, I was told by his great-
grandson, Maury Maverick, the congressman from San Antonio in New Deal
days.

Dobie heard this story, too, but didn't believe it. In *The Longhorns* he gives a
more prosaic explanation: that a caretaker of some four hundred cattle Maverick had taken in payment of a debt was too lazy to brand most of the calves. In
fact, Maverick never was a serious cattleman. He was a distinguished lawyer
and signer of the Texas Declaration of Independence from Mexico.

Incidentally, a brand had to be simple, easy to read at a distance, yet so
designed that a cattle thief could not easily change it to look like something
else. Brands are always read from left to right or top to bottom. Thus ⊥ is the
Tee Anchor, not the Anchor Tee.

him just between the horns. The beast collapsed instantly, and apparently painlessly.

The stunning was a chore Mr. Baxter always reserved for himself, because he didn't trust any ten-year-old to do it without hurting the steer. But from then on the job was all ours, under his laconic supervision. First Robert and I cut slits in the hind legs between bone and tendon, just above the hoofs. Into these we inserted the points of the spreader, a two-inch hickory stick about three feet long, sharpened at both ends. We tied a rope to the middle of the spreader and then threw the other end over the branch of a tree about ten feet above the ground. By tugging mightily, and with Mr. Baxter also tailing onto the rope if the steer was a heavy one, we hoisted it until its nose was about two feet above the ground. A gallon bucket went under the nose.

Either Robert or I took a skinning knife with a long, thin blade and jabbed it into the steer's throat at precisely the right place, about three inches above the jawbone. Nobody ever slashed a throat from side to side because that would have damaged too much of the hide. If the thrust hit the big throat artery, as it was supposed to, blood would spurt out in a quick fountain—we had to be nimble to dodge it—and then subside into a slow, viscous trickle that soon filled the bucket. Within half an hour the blood would congeal into a thick jelly. Some families would save this as a future ingredient for brawn and headcheese; we fed it to the chickens as a valuable supplement to their usual diet of milo maize and grasshoppers.

When the trickle stopped, we began the skinning. It started with a shallow incision exactly down the center line of the animal's belly from anus to jaw. Similar incisions were made in the inside of each leg, from the center cut to the hoofs. We were then ready to start peeling back the hide, with fingers and skinning knife, one boy working on each side. This was a more delicate operation than you might think. If the knife sliced too far into the body, it would leave bits of flesh and tallow clinging to the skin, which later had to scraped off. If it went too shallow, it was likely to puncture the hide, to Mr. Baxter's awesome wrath. But when everything went right, it came away inch by inch as neatly as the peel off an orange. After about three hours we had the hide spread on the ground under the carcass, hair side down, with tail, hoofs, and head still attached.

Next came an even more delicate operation—the removal of the viscera. If we were careful enough, all the innards came out in a single package, contained in a membrane like a cellophane wrapping. Lowering this onto the hide, we took out the heart, kidneys, sweetbreads, and marrow gut—an essential ingredient for son-of-a-bitch stew, a favorite dish in cattle country.* The rest went into a gulley a hundred yards away, to be disposed of by the crows and coyotes.

It usually took us another three hours or so to dismember the carcass into manageable chunks—haunches, forequarters, brisket, short ribs, and so on. What Aunt Myrtle needed for immediate use we took into the kitchen. The remainder, wrapped in brown-paper parcels, we loaded into Mr. Baxter's Model T Ford, for delivery to kinfolks (who added up to a big share of the population of Shamrock) and to the cold locker at the ice company downtown. Since beef was the main item in every meal, including breakfast, we could look forward to another butchering in three or four weeks.

Even ranch families rarely butcher their own meat these days, since it is easier to truck a yearling to the nearest slaughterhouse. Several of my Connecticut neighbors raise cattle, pigs, and sheep for their own tables, but so far as I know I am the only man in Guilford with any experience in home butchering. A good thing, too, my wife says. She regards the proceedings as barbarous, especially for ten-year-olds. It didn't seem so to Robert and me. We were not sentimental about our cattle, nor squeamish about the skinning and butchering. We felt we

---

* Making son-of-a-bitch stew may now be a lost art. I have never seen a written recipe, nor have I heard of anyone cooking it on the High Plains for many

were learning a new skill—a man's skill, far more interesting than our chores on horseback—and it provided the whiff of blood and violence that, Jung tells us, every small boy yearns for. We had no comic books to serve as surrogate.

We did have a few other diversions, such as a Tom Mix or Jack Holt Western film on Saturday nights; they struck us as extremely funny, because they bore no relation to the West we saw around us. And we had our garbage business.

Mr. Baxter believed in the eternal verities. Idleness Is the Thief of Time. Waste Not, Want Not. Work, for the Night Is Coming. The Devil Finds Business for Idle Hands. So he encouraged Robert and me into other enterprises when there were no cattle to move or horses to curry.

At that time, each household in Shamrock disposed of its own garbage, usually in a pit in the back lot or a nearby gulley. Robert knew where he could find four discarded wagon wheels

years. It was pre-eminently a dish suitable for a crew of five to twenty cowboys working a roundup or a trail drive, and camping at night around their chuck wagon. The cook—sometimes known as the crumb boss—made it by whittling chunks of fresh beef about the size of his thumb into a cast-iron Dutch oven. Then he added water, chopped up potatoes and onions, and (if the outfit was a comparatively luxurious one) a couple of cans of tomatoes. Finally he put in the sliced marrow-gut; this is a kind of branch, or appendix, attached to the cow's small intestine. It is not a hollow tube, like the intestines proper, but is solidly filled with a soft, white, marrow-like substance; it gave the stew a distinctive, though indescribable, flavor. The cook might also throw in some crumbled left-over biscuits to thicken the mixture, plus a generous helping of salt and pepper and maybe a chile or two. Then he would put the lid on the Dutch oven and set it on the campfire coals to simmer for a few hours. Aunt Myrtle often cooked such a stew in a kettle on her wood-burning kitchen range, but I never knew any other housewife who did.

Neither Mr. Baxter nor anyone else was ever able to explain to me why a cow had a marrow gut, or what its physiological function was. Maybe God just added it to the bovine equipment for culinary reasons.

Son-of-a-bitch stew got one cowboy into trouble. He worked for a foreman named Slim Carruthers, whom he heartily disliked from the beginning of the roundup because Carruthers was always complaining about the way the cowboy did his work. The third night out when the crew was gathered for supper, the cowboy ate his first helping of stew with a fast appetite and held out his plate to the cook.

"I sure would like another helping of that Carruthers stew," he said.

Naturally Carutters fired him on the spot.

and enough old lumber to make a wagon bed. After about a week's work putting the contraption together, we drafted a neighbor's burro—promptly christened Rosy—and were in business. Going from house to house, we collected any trash each family wanted to get rid of and hauled it to a gulley half a mile out of town. Our fees were reasonable—twenty-five cents a load—and we were providing the first organized garbage service the town ever had. It never occurred to us, or to anybody else, that there was anything undignified about our business. It certainly was better than cowboying.

TWO

Why the High Plains
Were Settled So Late

During one of my boyhood explorations of the country around Amarillo, Texas, where my family then lived, I came across an outcropping of grayish white rock that seemed to be made almost entirely of sea shells. I was so mystified that I took a sample and hurried home to ask my father how so many oysters had ever got to such a high-and-dry location. He identified the rock as caliche, which is indeed composed mostly of compressed shells, but had to refer me to the town library for its geological history.

What I found out was that for something like 150 million years, give or take an eon, the High Plains had been a sea bed, collecting layer upon layer of marine sediments. These eventually turned into shale, sandstone, slate, and several varieties of limestone, including my caliche. Entrapped within these strata were not only shells and fossilized fish, but also the organisms that created oil and natural gas. By the Triassic period, about

180 million years ago, the seas had evaporated, leaving a vast swamp infested with dinosaurs and toothy amphibious creatures resembling giant salamanders. Eons later, the same wrinkling of the earth's crust that thrust up the Rocky Mountains lifted the High Plains to roughly their present elevation, lying at the eastern foot of that range. There they received, for many thousands of years, the runoff from the mountains, carrying with it enough silt and gravel to cover the High Plains to a depth ranging from a few feet to five hundred. This mantle of debris filled in the creases and hollows that had resulted from the original violent upheaving of the marine strata, and thus gave the country its present appearance of an almost perfectly flat tableland.

If you fly from Dallas to Amarillo, you will know at once—about midway in the journey—when you reach the High Plains. Their eastern boundary is an irregular escarpment, rising abruptly from the lower prairies. Etched by centuries of erosion, this scarp was a formidable barrier to men on foot or horseback. At best they had to climb a steep, rubble-covered slope, and in most places the slope runs into a sheer cliff when it reaches the caprock. Hence, as the first white explorers discovered, it could be a military obstacle of considerable importance.

For thousands of years the High Plains resisted nearly all human settlement. They were hospitable only to buffalo—at an informed guess, at least 5 million of them—antelope, jack rabbits, prairie dogs (which are related to squirrels, not dogs), and such minor creatures as horny toads, squinch owls, and rattlesnakes. Climatically, they are the next thing to a desert; they get about twenty inches of rainfall in a good year, and bad years come pretty often. Almost nothing edible, therefore, grows there naturally—a few plums and wild grape along the creek banks, and that's about all.

Streams are few and far apart. Only three rivers cross the

High Plains in their Texas and Oklahoma heartland, all running from west to east: the Red River, with several forks, to the south; the Canadian River (which has nothing to do with Canada) in about the middle; and the Cimarron to the north. "River" is a rather grandiose term for such streams. For much of their length and at most times of the year, when you come to one of them you will see no water. It will look like a long ribbon of sand, perhaps a quarter of a mile wide. But often as not this is quicksand, because water seeps below the surface. Any man or heavy animal that stumbled into it might disappear in minutes.

A man on foot who strayed far from these rivers and their few little tributaries was in constant danger of death from thirst, aggravated by heat and drying winds. There was no shade. As late as my own boyhood, you could travel hundreds of miles without seeing any vegetation higher than your knees—nothing but sagebrush, grama grass, and an assortment of prickly shrubs.

For these reasons, the Indians who lived in the more hospitable foothills of the Rockies, or on the better-watered prairies to the east, seldom ventured onto this high plateau—until they got horses, sometime after 1541. To hunt antelope on foot was impossible, and jack rabbits and prairie dogs were elusive and unrewarding prey. Hunting buffalo on foot with lance and arrows was difficult and dangerous, although the Indians probably harvested some from the fringes of the great herd by setting grass fires, thereby stampeding the beasts over a cliff.

The tribes that visited the High Plains never attempted any permanent settlement, except in one place—the valley of the Canadian River. Archeologists differ about the date, but there is some reason to think that the first settlers arrived about fifteen thousand years ago. From where, nobody knows. Very little else is known about them either, except that they established the oldest industry in America. It was a quarry and flint-working factory on Alibates Creek, a tributary of the Canadian.*

The reason the first settlers chose that site was a deposit of prime flint—the most valuable of treasures to Paleolithic man. It was the raw material for their spear points, arrowheads, hide scrapers, and various domestic tools. Since the Alibates deposit is the only significant source of flint within hundreds of miles, the people who discovered and worked it had a virtually priceless monopoly. They are known today as the "Clovis people," because what appear to be the earliest points made from Alibates flint were first found near Clovis, New Mexico.

One of the few things we know about them is that they were hard workers. The flint they found was in the form of lumps or nodules, ranging from the size of a walnut to the size of a skull. These lumps were embedded, apparently at random, in hard dolomite limestone lying under a few inches of topsoil or exposed where the creek had cut the soil away. They were formed by a process of seepage, which geologists have tried to explain to me but which I have never fully understood. The flint is much harder than the dolomite, as hard as glass. The Alibates variety is, in fact, a form of agate, like the marbles prized by every small boy. It has a special quality: it can be split into bladelike flakes with a stone hammer, and these can then be shaped and sharpened by flaking with a pressure-point tool, such as a deer or buffalo horn. Some of them were fashioned with exquisite care, almost as if they were jewels. And, curiously, some of the older points—made, say, ten thousand years ago—were more delicately worked than the lance- and arrowheads made by Indians of historic times. The Clovis people both quarried the flint out of its dolomite matrix, a formidable task with the crude tools available to them, and worked up finished products for their own needs and for trading.

* Named after Ali Bates, the cowboy who rediscovered it late in the last century.

They were followed by people of other cultures: by Folsom man, who improved the quality of flint workmanship; by Archaic Indians; and finally by a comparatively civilized group who built two pueblos out of rock and adobe near the flint mine. Apparently they hacked away at their work as diligently as any of their predecessors, because the site today contains more than five hundred quarry pits, some of them twenty feet wide—the labor of many generations. In the early thirties my uncle Joe Williams held an oil lease on a tract of land along Alibates Creek, and his family and mine often went there for picnics. The youngsters paddled in the stream and looked for arrowheads, while the women gathered wild plums for jam. We found few perfect points—naturally enough, since they would have been used or traded—but we did pick up many arrowheads broken in the making, plus innumerable flint chips. Most of this industrial waste was strewn around a place we called the Factory, a strip of land about two hundred yards long under the bank of the creek, where the Indians could work their flint in shelter from the wind, yet close to the quarry holes. It was a lonely place when we visited it; I never saw anyone else there except our two families. Today it is a national monument, attracting a steady tourist traffic.

From the earliest times the trade in flint, both nodules and shaped points, seems to have been astonishingly widespread. At several locations in New Mexico and Arizona, archeologists have found the skeletons of animals that have long been extinct, such as the mammoth and giant bison—and among the bones were the spearheads that presumably killed them, shaped from the distinctive, multicolored Alibates agate. Moreover, among the sixteen thousand artifacts found at one of the Alibates pueblos were many items that could have come there only as trade goods from far-distant tribes: sea shells from the Gulf Coast, obsidian from the Yellowstone country, turquoise and pottery from Arizona and New Mexico, and red pipestone from Minnesota. What route it traveled is impossible to guess.

When the pueblo dwellers, sometimes known as the Plains Village Indians, arrived at the site—perhaps a thousand years ago—the climate may well have been more humid than it is today, for there are indications that they were farmers as well as miners and flint workers. Indeed, half a dozen other pueblos have been found further up the Canadian, where there was no flint. Their inhabitants evidently lived by hunting and farming alone, without benefit of industrial employment. All of the pueblos, including those at Alibates Creek, were abandoned about A.D. 1450, probably because of a prolonged drought. Nevertheless, the quarries continued to be worked sporadically by nomadic tribes, such as the Comanches, Apaches, and Kiowa, well into the nineteenth century. Some bands probably made their winter encampments along the creek, chipping flint in their spare time.

About a century after the Alibates people left, the Spaniards reached the High Plains. The first of them were the cavalry of Francisco Vásquez de Coronado, who crossed the Panhandle in 1541 in search of the fabled Seven Cities of Cibola. They found no cities, no gold, no silver, nor anything else that could tempt a Spaniard to stay there. But they, or later Spanish explorers, left behind some horses—lost, strayed, or stolen.*

They felt right at home, because the Southwest was much like the country in Spain and North Africa where Spanish warhorses originated. They were of Arab and barb stock, small, spirited, and hardy. They flourished so well that herds of wild horses were common throughout the Great Plains within a century of the Coronado and De Soto expeditions.

---

* There is no firm evidence that Coronado's horses were the first to populate the High Plains, although, except for the native American horses that had become extinct millions of years before the arrival of the first Indians, they certainly were the first to set hoof there. We do know that Hernando De Soto abandoned some worn-down horses on his ill-fated expedition to Oklahoma in 1541. And many others got loose or fell into Indian hands in Mexico after Cortes's conquest.

With horses, the Indians found it practical for the first time to live on the High Plains. They could kill buffalo and move from one watering place to another in relative safety. No permanent buildings were needed, since the tribes who populated this country were strictly nomadic—moving their tent villages whenever they needed to find fresh grass, or to follow the buffalo. Their teepees were made, naturally, of buffalo hide, and were carried from place to place on travois—two poles, tied at one end on each side of a horse's pack saddle, with the other ends trailing on the ground. The squaws and children were responsible for lashing their hides and household belongings onto such poles at moving time, and setting up the next camp.

The horse Indians who moved into the High Plains were the toughest in North America. Anything that survived there had to be tough. The dominant tribe was the Comanches, who came down from the mountains to the west. They were short, stocky, mean, and predators by nature. Their prey was the buffalo; the gentler and more sedentary tribes, such as the Hopi farmers in New Mexico; the Mexicans in what is now south Texas and below the Rio Grande; and any stranger who ventured into their domain.

It is customary among most modern novelists and film makers to picture all Indians as the innocent victims of white rapacity and greed. They are commonly portrayed as Rousseauistic children of nature, living in harmony with their environment and each other, until this idyll was disrupted by white invaders.

That may have been almost true of some of the more civilized tribes, such as the Cherokees and Mandans. But nothing could be further from the truth about the Comanches, or their neighbors on the Great Plains, the Apaches and Kiowas.

Walter Prescott Webb described them as "by nature more ferocious, implacable, and cruel than the other tribes." Francis F. McKinney called them "the most terrible savages of the plains," who "killed and captured more whites than any other Western Indians and stole more horses and cattle." Colonel Richard Irving Dodge, writing in 1877, told how they had developed torture into an art. "Cruelty is both an amusement and a study," he said.

So much pleasure is derived from it that an Indian is constantly thinking out new devices of torture, and how to prolong to the utmost those already known. His anatomical knowledge of the most sensitive portions of the human frame is wonderfully accurate; and the amount of beating, cutting, slashing, and burning he will make a human body undergo without affecting the vital powers is astonishing.*

Such treatment sometimes went on for two or three days before the prisoner died—and the Comanche squaws were particularly expert at torment. The great majority of their victims were, of course, other Indians, with whom the Comanches kept up virtually continuous warfare, but they were glad to snap up a Mexican or Texan when they could. Whites caught in an Indian fight soon learned to save their last bullets for themselves.

The Comanches expected the same treatment if they were captured, so they never surrendered until they were too wounded to resist further. In 1860 Major George H. Thomas— later one of the most successful Union generals in the Civil War—was pursuing a Comanche raiding party with a command of twenty-five cavalrymen near the Clear Fork of the Brazos River in Texas. The Indians told off one warrior to serve as rear guard while they tried to escape with their herd of stolen horses. What happened next is related by McKinney, Thomas's biographer:

Suddenly the Indian rear guard slipped off his horse, kicked off his moccasins,† dropped to one knee, and unslung his arrows. The troopers, still mounted, charged on him in a mass, firing as they moved. A

* Richard Irving Dodge, *The Hunting Grounds of the Great West* (London: Chatto & Windus, 1877).
† The customary Comanche gesture to indicate that he would run no further and proposed to die on the spot.

hail of bullets filled the air around him. More than twenty of them took effect.

A charging horseman offers only a small target—face, shoulders, arms, and legs—the rest of his body being masked from a dismounted man by the horse's head, neck, and chest. A galloping horse could cover the effective range of an arrow in fifteen to twenty seconds. Yet the Indian's arrows found those moving targets four times. They inflicted one face wound [on Thomas], one shoulder wound, and two leg wounds on four different men. These were all aimed shots and the rapidity of his fire was extraordinary. When the fight closed to hand-to-hand combat the Indian inflicted two more casualties with his lance but, weakened by his numerous wounds, he lacked the strength to drive home his steel. The odds against him were greater than those faced by Custer and by the defenders of the Alamo.*

The Comanches were not only ruthless and brave, they were better warriors than any white troops, Mexican or American, that they met until about 1840. They were better mounted, better riders, better tacticians, and better armed. In addition to his fourteen-foot lance and bull-hide shield, each warrior carried a short bow, made of ash or bois d'arc, and up to a hundred arrows. These he could fire at full gallop fast enough to keep one in the air at all times, and with enough force to go clear through a man or buffalo at close range.

In contrast, the first white men to encounter the Comanches were armed with single-shot, muzzle-loading cap-and-ball rifles, which could not be reloaded on horseback and took at least a minute to reload on the ground. In that time an Indian could ride three hundred yards and get off twenty arrows. The white man might also carry one or two single-shot pistols, equally hard to reload. His only advantage was that his weapons had a greater range—and that was seldom enough to offset the Indian's greater mobility and fire power.

Small wonder, then, that both Mexicans and Americans usually avoided the High Plains. There was a trail, known as

* Francis F. McKinney, *Education in Violence: The Life of George H. Thomas* (Detroit: Wayne State University Press. 1961).

the Great Spanish Road, along the Canadian River valley, but it could be prudently traveled only by large, well-armed parties or by traders who had made a tenuous peace with the Comanches. One of these was William Bent, who built an adobe trading post on the north side of the Canadian, in what is now Hutchinson County, about 1843. He operated it for five or six years, primarily as a receiving point for horses and mules that the Indians had stolen in Mexico and South Texas. These he sold in turn at his main trading post, Bent's Fort, in Colorado. Long after he abandoned his Hutchinson County building, two famous battles with the Indians occurred at or near its site. Known as the First and Second Battles of Adobe Walls, the first was fought by a party led by Kit Carson in 1864, the second by a band of buffalo hunters ten years later. In neither of them could the whites claim a clear-cut victory.

Rather than risk the Canadian River trail, most travelers swung around the High Plains in long detours: the Mexicans to the south, the Americans to the north along a route that led from Independence, Missouri, to Santa Fe by way of Bent's Fort and the Raton Pass. For the Comanche country could not be permanently settled, or even traveled in safety, until the Indians were cleared out. And that was impossible until the Americans got repeating weapons.

Samuel Colt finally provided them. He invented his six-shot revolving pistol at the age of sixteen, whittling out a wooden model while he was serving as a sailor on a voyage from Boston to Calcutta. He took out his first patent in 1835, and according to Webb in his classic history, *The Great Plains,** revolvers were imported into Texas to arm the Rangers in 1839. The first model was not entirely satisfactory, so a Ranger captain, Samuel H. Walker, went to New York to suggest certain improvements to Colt: a heavier caliber, a simpler reloading mecha-

*Boston: Ginn & Co., 1931.

nism, and a trigger guard. These the inventor eagerly accepted, naming the improved model "the Walker."

The Indians encountered this weapon for the first time on June 8, 1844, in the Battle of the Pedernales, not far from Lyndon B. Johnson's future birthplace. There a party of about seventy Comanches attacked fourteen Rangers, led by John C. Hays, the commander of the corps. To their astonishment, the Comanches lost thirty warriors, while the Rangers suffered only a few casualties, the exact number unrecorded.* The Texans at last had a weapon superior to the Comanche's bow.

Colt also invented a repeating rifle, but it was less successful than his pistol, and really efficient multishot cavalry carbines did not come into widespread use until the Civil War. By that time, however, both the Rangers and the regular army were too busy elsewhere to attempt a conquest of the Comanche stronghold on the High Plains.

That conquest finally took place in 1874. The federal army, recuperated from the war, mounted a major campaign, with five columns converging on the High Plains from different directions. General Philip Sheridan later appraised it as the most successful of the campaigns against the Indians. Although the troops fought some twenty-five skirmishes, casualties were not high on either side; and in the end the Comanches and their sometimes foes, sometimes allies, the Apaches and Kiowas were rounded up and herded north to assigned reservations in Oklahoma.

A brutal eviction of people from their ancestral homes? Well, yes, I guess so, by modern standards. But these same Indians had evicted many Mexicans and Americans from *their* homes, and they did not send their victims to reservations. They sent them to the Hereafter, keeping scalps as mementos. I went to

---

* An account of this engagement was written by a remote relative of mine, John C. Caperton, and included in his manuscript "Sketch of the Life of John C. Hays." A transcript is now in the University of Texas archives.

college with many Apaches, Comanches, and Kiowas at the University of Oklahoma in the early thirties, not to mention a good many Sac-Fox and Osages. Some of them became close friends, but I never was able to grieve a whole lot over the fate of their ancestors.

By 1875—the key date in the history of the High Plains—the chief obstacle to settlement was gone. Trouble with the Indians wasn't over yet, since the outbreaks of Geronimo and lesser marauders were still to come. But Fort Elliott was established in Wheeler County, close to the Oklahoma border, to guard against any mass return of the tribes. Permanent settlers in substantial numbers began to arrive the same year.

One other considerable obstacle remained—the buffalo. He had many virtues. He was hardier than cattle against extremes of climate, fought off wolves and coyotes more effectively, grew larger, and converted grass into protein more efficiently. But he was utterly intractable. A stupid, stubborn animal, the buffalo was impossible to herd or to confine with any fencing then known. Systematic ranching was impossible until the buffalo—like the Indian—was removed from the range.

The slaughter of the buffalo, the most massive in history, took only a few years. The hunters had two incentives, aside from clearing the range. Some of them, including Buffalo Bill Cody, were hired to provide cheap meat for the crews that were then pushing the railway tracks west into the Great Plains. But most of them were interested only in the hides to make an exceptionally tough leather, especially useful for industrial belting. (Most factory machinery at that time was turned by leather belts, running off a central steam-driven shaft.) Buffalo skins also became fashionable both in England and the Eastern United States, for floor coverings and for carriage lap robes.

There was nothing sporting about buffalo hunting. Unlike the nervous antelope, the buffalo herds permitted hunters to approach on foot or horseback to short rifle range. When the first one was dropped, the others did not run away; instead they gathered around the carcass, sniffing it in apparent curiosity, and so became easy targets in turn. It was no trick for an average marksman to kill more than fifty an hour. The usual weapon was a Sharps rifle, throwing a heavy 50-caliber bullet that would knock the great beasts down with one shot.

I saw what one of these balls could do when I was a police reporter for the *Daily Oklahoman* in 1933. Pretty Boy Floyd and his partner, George Birdwell, were then doing a brisk trade in robbing banks. One day they decided to knock off the only bank in the little all-Negro town of Boley, not far from Oklahoma City. The cashier, who was also the president, handed over his small stock of cash meekly enough. But as Floyd and Birdwell got in their car to drive away, he reached behind the counter, picked up an old Sharps, rested it on the counter for a steady aim, and let fly at the back of Birdwell's head. When I arrived on the scene an hour or so later, to interview the cashier and view the body, I found that Birdwell's head had practically disappeared. Bullet wounds were no novelty to me, since I had to cover many suicides and murders during that depression year, but Birdwell's was the most revolting I have ever seen, before or since. (Floyd, as usual, had escaped.)

When my mother and her family started their homestead at Dozier in 1891, the buffalo were gone—some 5 million of them slaughtered in little more than a decade. But their bones and droppings still littered the prairie. One of my mother's chores was to gather dried buffalo and cow chips for fuel, since firewood was virtually nonexistent. And she used to tell me how her father and brother would collect the bones, during their first cash-hungry years in Texas, for shipment by the wagonload to Eastern fertilizer factories.

THREE

Reluctant Pioneer

George Sylvester Caperton came to Texas reluctantly. He had been quite content with his life in Alabama. There he had inherited two homesteads, one on the Tennessee River at Caperton's Ferry, about twenty miles south of Chattanooga, the other on Sand Mountain a couple of miles east of the ferry. At the mountain farm he and his wife raised ten children. (An eleventh was born after they moved west.) Their home was comfortable enough for that time—in fact, more comfortable than any home he would know later. It was a log cabin evidently built in 1849, the date carved on the stone chimney. Its walls were constructed mainly of squared walnut logs, some of them from trees that must have measured four feet through the butt. (If such a tree could be found today, it would be worth at least $5,000 at any veneer factory. That was the price for which the Capertons sold both their farms when they decided to move to the High Plains.) When I visited the place for the only time, in the late thirties, it was still a tight, sturdy cabin, although the current tenants obviously weren't putting much effort into its upkeep.

To my mother, the last of the Caperton children born there, it seemed almost luxurious—and probably was, in comparison with the homes of their neighbors. In one of several memoranda that she wrote about her early life, she described it as a "plantation," a rather grandiose term for a hardscrabble Appalachian hill farm. But the house did have two stories and an attic, plus porches front and back and a big kitchen with dining room in an L at the rear. A wide, open hall, or breezeway, pierced the first story, connecting the two porches and providing a large space for kids to play in rainy weather. Because it was cool and shady, the breezeway was also generally cluttered with chickens and hound dogs, including Molly Golightly, reputed to be the best coon dog in northern Alabama.

The main room on the first floor was the parlor, opened only on special occasions. My mother described it as

well furnished with figured carpet, red velvet drapes on shuttered windows, an ebony-wood upright Baldwin piano, cherry wood tables with marble tops, chairs and sofa upholstered in horse hair, a book case and a what-not. The latter held trinkets of ivory and gold and precious keepsakes. Books were well read. *Aesop's Fables, Pilgrim's Progress,* and *Apples of Gold in Pictures of Silver* were some of the ones in our home. The Bible and the *Atlanta Constitution* were daily reading, as were other periodicals and magazines.

The farms produced enough to feed a large family reasonably well, though without much variety. Ordinarily the only meat on the table was either chicken or pork—fresh in the summer, cured in the smokehouse for winter. Since there was no refrigeration, it was not practical to keep beef for more than a few days, and even a dozen hearty eaters could not finish a whole cow in that time. George Caperton and his elder sons loved to hunt, and they brought in some small game nearly every week—squirrel, possum, wild turkey, and an occasional deer. The younger children gathered wild berries; churned butter and stored it in the spring house, where running water kept the crocks fairly cool; and helped in the vegetable garden. Both sweet and Irish potatoes were stored in trenches for winter use, cabbage was made into sauerkraut, and cucumbers and some fruit was pickled; home canning was then unknown. Corn meal and lye hominy, made with wood ashes in a big cast-iron laundry kettle, were staple items; since white flour had to be purchased, it was used sparingly, for cakes and light biscuits or a loaf of bread on special occasions. Oranges were a rarity, appearing only at Christmas—one for each child.

What little cash the family used came from the hogs and corn—usually only a dozen or so bushels—raised in excess of their own needs. And from the ferry tolls.

The ferry was a large raft, fastened by pulley to a cable across the Tennessee River. With a steering oar, the one-man crew could maneuver it so that the current would push it across the river in either direction. The main labor was lowering the cable to the river bottom whenever steamboats came along, sometimes several a day, sometimes one a week. At night and whenever else the ferry was out of operation, the cable was left on the bottom so an unexpected boat would not snap it. Raising it called for hard work at a windlass, since the cable was heavy.

Such work, I suspect, was generally done by one of the family Negroes, although the ferry itself was usually operated by Mr. Caperton or one of his elder sons. The Capertons owned slaves before the Civil War—perhaps a dozen, as far as I can make out from family remembrances. They were under the loose command of the senior man, Wesley, named after the evangelist. (Like the whites on the place, the blacks were staunch Methodists.) Evidently they had been inherited along with the land, since my mother is certain that none was ever bought or sold.

When George Caperton went off at the beginning of the war to join the Eighth Alabama Confederate Cavalry Regiment, in General Joe Wheeler's corps, he left the farms in Wesley's charge. (George was unmarried then, and his parents were too old for farm work.) With the help of the other slaves, Wesley took care of them well. Once a column of federal infantry, on its way to the Chickamauga battlefield nearby, crossed at Caperton's Ferry and paused for a brief rest at the farm on Sand Mountain. They harmed no one and looted nothing, although the soldiers did "borrow" a few fence rails to boil coffee. But the colonel did tell the Caperton slaves that they were free to leave. They thanked him respectfully, but none left. Indeed, they all stayed on after the war, living and working much as they had before emancipation. And when the Capertons moved to Texas, Wesley went along to help get them settled in their new home. He found the Panhandle lonesome and unwelcoming, however, and after a few years he returned to De Kalb County, Alabama.

My wife once remarked acidly, "Blacks and whites seemed to live as one big happy family, in which the blacks did most of the work." Certainly Mr. Caperton never became addicted to work. My mother was exaggerating when she said, "He never did a lick of work in his life until he got to Texas," but not much. During the war he had served faithfully, fighting in all of Wheeler's campaigns. His captain, Judge J. K. Miller of Talladega, Alabama, later wrote of him:

He, from the time of his enlistment at Jackson Co., Alabama April 16, 1861, at the age of twenty years, to the time of the surrender of the Army of The Tennessee by General Joseph E. Johnston at Greensboro, N.C., April 26, 1865, did not at any time desert the service of the Confederate States, and at all times fully performed all the high and trying duties of a true and gallant Confederate Cavalryman. . . .

(It was easier for a cavalryman than an infantryman to desert, and many did, at least temporarily, particularly in the last two years of the war. One who did not was considered noteworthy, if not a little foolish.)

After such exertions, George Caperton felt entitled to rest up for the rest of his life, and he reverted thankfully to a life of hunting, fishing in the Tennessee, and light spells at the ferry. Incidentally, his only wound in the war was a knife cut, inflicted by a fellow Confederate in a campfire brawl. He did lose the horse he took with him at enlistment but came home with a better one, a Morgan, captured from an Ohio trooper. Perhaps because of his quick temper, or his devotion to captured whiskey, he was never promoted above private.

For Mr. Caperton, alas, sometimes drank, as the saying went, more than was good for him. (My Capterton kin will never forgive me for recording this, but it is the truth; and it has considerable bearing on later events in this book.) Worse yet, he encouraged his two elder sons, Charlie and Claude, to drink with him. Charlie told me, many years later, about the time when they had taken a jug of corn whiskey as payment in kind for a ferry fee.

"We had a few nips during the course of the afternoon, and come dark after we had tied up the ferry and lowered the cable, we had another. Then we started the long walk home up the Sand Mountain road. It was winter, and a rarely hard one for that part of the country, so maybe we took some additional reinforcements against the cold. Then we came to a creek, about ten feet wide, that was frozen over. After some discussion, we decided it was too dangerous to carry the jug across, because we might slip and break it. The safe thing, we agreed, would be to slide it across the ice to the other side. Unfortunately, Father slid it too hard, and it broke against a rock on the far bank.

"Of course we didn't want all that good whiskey to go to waste, so we laid down on our bellies and lapped up what we could. Somehow—I don't remember just how it happened—we all three froze solid to the ice, and couldn't get up until mother came looking for us an hour or two later. She gave us all a good tongue-lashing, and wouldn't pull us loose until we promised never to do such a fool thing again. We didn't. Or leastways we never got stuck to the ice again."

Charlie died in 1941 in Washington, D.C., at the age of sixty-nine. On his deathbed he told me that his fatal bout of pneumonia had been brought on by drinking too much, and advised me to take solemn warning.

In spite of such incidents, the marriage of George Caperton and Mary Helen Smith Caperton was a happy one. Both parents, and all their children, loved to dance, and did it well. Saturday afternoon dancing and singing parties, in the breezeway, were frequent, with Mother Caperton playing the piano in the parlor, and the children contributing something on banjos, mandolins, jew's-harps, and harmonicas. Often neighbors and the Negro children joined in. "Music," my mother wrote, "was a big part of our lives."

Nevertheless, Mary Helen Caperton was not as satisfied as her husband with their life on Sand Mountain. For one thing, the local schools were poor, and private tutors were too expensive. She set great store on education, since she herself had attended "the female academy" in Cave Springs, Georgia, at a time when few girls ever got beyond grade school.

Moreover, she foresaw that the Alabama farms and ferry, though adequate for one family's living, would not go far if they eventually had to be divided among ten children. Some of them would have to become tenant farmers, a fate she abhorred. (It never occurred to any of them that they might learn professions or move to factory jobs in some city. Farming was the only life they knew, or aspired to.)

So Mrs. Caperton determined to take her family West, where land was cheap and plentiful enough for the whole brood, and where good schools—through God's mercy, she trusted—would soon be available. In character, she was much the stronger partner. "An extraordinary woman, small of stature but a mental giant, strong and patient," is how one of her children later described her. When she made up her mind, her husband's demurs were futile.

In 1891, then, they started for the High Plains, recently

opened to settlement and the goal of many a Confederate veteran. Texas was then offering some of its school lands—that is, the part of the public domain set aside to finance schools—for sale at $1.25 an acre. Much of the school land on the market was located in Wheeler County, which originally included most of the north part of the Panhandle, though it later was subdivided into several counties. The fact that it was named after Mr. Caperton's old commander may have been an extra attraction; in any case, that is where they headed.

With them went the family of George Caperton's brother, John Hardy Caperton. He had also inherited property on Sand Mountain, and had married a sister of Mary Helen Smith Caperton. The children of the two families were therefore double cousins, and had been playmates all their lives. It was not surprising, then, that the George and John Capertons decided to migrate together, preserving a relationship precious to both families and providing mutual support.

After selling their farms, they chartered a train—one car for parents and children, another for furniture and farm implements, and a third for livestock and Wesley, who was to feed and water them en route. The animals included two spans of good mules, a few milk cows, and Gussie Dasher, Mary Helen Caperton's thoroughbred bay mare. She was to prove the most indispensable member of the party.

Claude and Charlie had gone ahead to scout out the land. They finally picked a half-section—320 acres—near Dozier Creek, in what is now Collingsworth County. Its main asset was the creek's sweet water, a bare trickle running only for a mile or so from a small spring to the Salt Fork of the Red River. The river itself, like most of that country's few streams, was so loaded with alkali and gypsum that it was almost undrinkable.

The chartered train took the band of settlers as far as Childress, a new, raw hamlet about sixty miles south of the claim the boys had staked out. There they left most of their possessions for the time being and started across the prairie with two wagons, their livestock, a few tools and boards, and a scanty supply of food. Since there was no road and the gulleys were unbridged, the trip took them three days.

When they reached Dozier Creek, what they saw was daunting, but there was no way to turn back. In Alabama, 320 acres would have been a big farm; here it seemed only a tiny patch in the middle of a vast semidesert, stretching flat as the ocean as far as the eye could reach. No tree, no habitation, no human being had they seen since leaving Childress. Nothing to see but dried-up buffalo grass and sagebrush. Nothing to hear except the ceaseless wind.

After the first few hours of discouragement, the two families decided that their plight might not be quite hopeless. They filled a barrel with water from the creek. The women started to cook a meal and make beds, in and under the wagons. The men started to dig, on a little knoll rising a foot or two above the prairie.

As Claude and Charlie had learned on their scout, digging was the only practical way to make a first home. Freighting lumber from the Childress railhead would have taken months, even if they could have afforded it; and winter was only weeks away. First the men cut the sod into squares, about two feet on each side and eight inches thick, and removed it from a site twenty feet long and fifteen feet wide. This they stacked to one side, while they took out dirt to a depth of five feet. Then along the edges of the digging they laid up the sod into walls rising two and a half feet above the ground. Using what little lumber they brought with them, they framed a door on the south side—away from the winter winds—and window openings in the east and west walls. Boards and poles made a roof, sloped enough to shed rain—if it ever came—and these were covered with brush, dirt, and more sod. Five steps cut in the earth led down to the door. Packed earth served as a floor, and muslin covered the windows until they could haul glass from Childress some weeks later.

This structure, known as a "dugout" or "soddy," was completed in a few days. It was crowded, but more comfortable than you might think because it was cool in summer and warm in winter. In the beginning all cooking was done over a campfire of sagebrush or cow and buffalo chips, although a fireplace and chimney were eventually added at the back of the house. While the weather held fair, the older children continued to sleep in or under the wagons. By winter, additional dugouts had been built and joined together by connecting doors, like a railway tenement—three for the George Caperton family and probably the same number for his brother's, a little distance away.

"We just kept digging," my mother said, "like prairie dogs."

While most of the men worked on the soddies, two headed the wagons back to Childress for more of their possessions— the first of many weary trips that finally wore a sort of road across the plains; it ran roughly where State Highway 83 does today. During their rest periods, the diggers shot jack rabbits, and on rare occasions an antelope, for meat. When that wasn't enough, they butchered a cow—usually a maverick,* driven back from one of their exploratory rides on Gussie Dasher.

In this climate, unlike Alabama's, every morsel of fresh beef could be preserved. You simply cut it into thin strips and hung these on a fence or clothesline for a few days. The sun and the drying wind turned the meat into jerky, which lasts indefinitely and tastes something like tough chipped beef.

The women planted vegetable gardens—and, inevitably, a few flowers by the door—hauling water by the barrelful to keep them going between the infrequent rains. After a few trips to Childress they also had chickens and a brood sow, plus a few sacks of flour, corn meal, and dried beans. Later they got boards to floor the dugout and line the inner walls, and curtains to partition off sleeping quarters.

But the Capertons soon learned that they could not survive

* These strays were presumably from the Rocking Chair Ranche (sic), which had used the Salt Fork country as part of its range (unfenced and unowned) until the settlers came in.

by ranching on a half-section. In country where it took at least twenty acres to graze a single cow, moderate-sized ranches ran to fifteen sections, and big ones into the hundreds. The family did not have enough money to buy an adequate spread, fence it, and build up a herd. So the two elder sons, Claude and Charlie, left for Colorado, where, they had heard, the Cripple Creek gold strike was providing plenty of jobs at good pay. For two years they worked in and around Ouray, in the mines and at a variety of odd jobs—including carpentry and helping to run a livery stable—and the wages they sent home kept the family going through those first years. When the boys returned, they took up land of their own and helped their parents build a small frame house, stripping the dugouts of boards to add to the new lumber hauled from Childress.

That house is still standing, though no longer in the family's ownership; and at last it is comfortably shaded by the cottonwoods and other trees my grandfather and grandmother planted. Nearby is another house, built by Claude when he got married. When I last visited it, in 1975, his second wife, Maxie, was still living there, alone but undaunted at a wondrous old age. The dugouts had long since crumbled away, and the corral where Robert and I had practiced roping was gone, too. Less than half a dozen other houses, some of them boarded up, were left of the once promising settlement of Dozier. It no longer has the post office, once run as a sideline by three generations of Capertons.

I have recounted the founding of the settlement in some detail, because it was typical of the beginnings of many other High Plains hamlets—such as Muleshoe, Ida, Ware, Gruver, and Samnorwood—and in some cases of their endings, too. There was little romance about it, in spite of what you may have read in a hundred Western novels. There was little violence, either. One of the most durable Western legends is that the big cattlemen resented and discouraged the coming of the little ranchers and farmers, who fenced in the previously open and rent-free range. Some intentional discouragement did occur at Tascosa, as I shall note later, and brief, sporadic range wars flared up in parts of New Mexico and Wyoming. But such occurrences were entirely untypical. None of my family ever had any trouble with the big cattlemen, nor did any other family that I knew.

On the contrary, the owners and cow hands of the large ranches—notably the Rocking Chair, the RO, the JA, the Mill Iron, and the Tee Anchor—were unfailingly helpful and friendly to the newcomers. They frequently brought the Capertons orphan calves that they could have branded for themselves, helped locate quarter horses for sale at a decent price, and gave a hand in any emergency. If someone broke a leg or got bitten by a rattlesnake or hooked by a peevish bull, the axiomatic resort was to "put a kid on a horse." He or she would light out for the nearest line camp or chuck wagon, and bring back somebody who knew what to do. A competent cow hand could set a leg or cauterize a snakebite as well as he could grease a windmill or break an untamed pony, and was glad to undertake any of these chores on request.

Of course, the presence of five pretty daughters at the Caperton dugout may have had something to do with all this cordiality. Women were scarce on the high plains, so the cowboys—and their bosses—were eager to ride twenty miles or more for a dance, a meal, or just to sit and talk a while. Mrs. Caperton fed them all, keeping open house day and night. And when a kid on a horse called for her, she would set off at any hour on Gussie Dasher to deliver a baby or lay out a corpse or cook a meal for a sick neighbor.

She never had to treat a bullet wound. At the risk of unwelcome disillusionment to Western fans, I have to record that cowboys did not shoot each other at the drop of an uncautious remark. In fact, by 1890 they seldom carried guns. In ordinary ranch work a revolver and cartridge belt were heavy, hot, in the way, and useless. A pistol's range was too short to kill a coyote or lobo, and the myth that you could turn a stampeding herd of cattle by firing a six-shooter is simply ridiculous. Such tactics would have made the beasts even more hysterical. Most range outfits did carry a rifle in the chuck wagon, for wolves or coyotes, and sometimes a revolver for killing cows that broke a leg or calves born on a trail drive. (The babies couldn't keep up, and when they dropped behind their mothers tried to stay with them, unless the calves were shot. Rather late in the trail-driving days, some outfits added a calf wagon to pick up anything born on the march.)

George Caperton never owned a revolver after he came to Texas. His only firearm was a curious one—half rifle, half shotgun; that is, it had two barrels, fired by percussion caps, one that took shot, the other ball. It is now in the Panhandle-Plains Historical Museum in Canyon. As far as other guns went, my grandfather Fischer had a Navy Colt he brought back from the Civil War, but he kept it merely as a souvenir. My only relative who did carry a gun, on occasion, was my uncle, Charles Caperton. He had got interested in marksmanship while he was in Colorado, and finally became proficient enough with a handgun to represent the United States in several international matches. Even when he was an old man, living in Washington, D.C., he used to practice in the coal cellar of the boardinghouse run by his wife, Cate. On a visit to my wife and me, shortly after we were married, he startled her by tossing his .45 on the sofa, remarking that it was uncomfortable in his shoulder holster in hot weather. He had brought it along that day, I'm pretty sure, just to see what a Scottish girl's reaction would be. Charlie fired thousands of rounds in his lifetime, but none of them in anger.

The big ranches did keep guns of all kinds at their headquarters, and issued them to their hands in rare emergencies, such as an outbreak of cow thefts or the pursuit of an outlaw such as Billy the Kid. When a trail herd reached Dodge City or Abilene, the cowboys would usually put on guns, partly to show off, partly because these towns were full of toughs who would rob a drunk—which most hands aspired to be, soon after arrival. Some wore guns on routine visits to Childress, Clarendon, or Tascosa, for similar reasons. But the more prudent did not. As my grandfather Fischer once told me:

"It is never smart to carry a gun, unless you are sure you can use it better than anyone you are likely to meet. If you do, never pull it unless you mean to shoot instantly. And if you must shoot, aim to kill."

Years later, while I was a newspaper reporter, I found it necessary—on the advice of a county sheriff—to carry a pistol for a few weeks. But I certainly could not have used it with any skill, and fortunately never had to take it out of its holster.

The unromantic truth is that most cowboys were no more adept with firearms than I was; and when a shooting scrape did occur it was as likely to be comic as tragic. Witness the following story, written down by my Uncle Claude and quoted by Laura V. Hamner in her *Short Grass and Longhorns*.* The two principals mentioned were parties to a long-standing dispute about where the county seat of Collingsworth County should be located:

E. E. McCollister had been given a post office at Aberdeen and I went there for Frank King's and my mail; we batched together my first year in Bradley Flat. . . . I saw Ed Tomlinson and Jack Drew meet. Drew's father ran the Rocking Chair Ranche. Tomlinson drew his pistol and began firing. Drew put spurs to his horse and ran a mile to the ranch house with Ed close behind him. Drew's mother came out of the ranch house with a rifle and gave it to Jack. Ed ran one-fourth of a mile to his dugout and ran inside. Jack proceeded to shoot twenty or thirty holes through the shack. I do not recall any further trouble between them.

* Norman: University of Oklahoma Press, 1943.

FOUR

Colonel Goodnight and the British Connection

In 1928, when I was eighteen years old, I became the most junior reporter on the Amarillo *Globe-News*. Gene Howe, the editor and a close-fisted one, hired me unwillingly, only because it struck him as the cheapest solution to what he saw as a problem.

At the time I was also coeditor of the high school newspaper, and thus in close touch with what the other students were doing. Noticing that the *Globe-News* was carrying little high school news, I suggested to Howe that I might fill the gap by contributing occasional items on a piecework basis. He agreed, offering me fifteen cents a column inch for any material the paper published. Nearly every evening from then on I turned in three or four items to the city editor, Joe Cannon, who printed nearly all of them. As instructed, I clipped my items and pasted them together in a long strip. At the end of the

45

month I took this to Cannon for payment. He measured it, did a bit of figuring, and whistled.

"Jesus Christ," he said, "I hadn't realized that we were printing so much high school news. This adds up to thirty-two dollars, which is almost as much as we pay some full-time reporters. The old man will be sore as hell."

He walked across the editorial room to the editor's office, a glass-enclosed cubicle from which Howe could watch everything that went on at the copy desk and the reporters' typewriters; if he saw anyone sitting idle or engaged in a possibly unnecessary conversation, he was quick to charge out with a reproof. A moment after Cannon had entered, I heard something between a bellow and a moan of pain coming over the glass partition. Cannon came out grinning.

"The boss says it's outrageous to pay a kid that kind of money. He doesn't want to stop the high school news because I told him lots of people read it. But he ordered me to take you off piecework and put you on a regular salary of fifteen dollars a month."

That struck me as an outrageous deal, but I said I would accept if the job would last through the three summer months when school was closed. That was all right with Joe, because Howe kept him short of reporters summer and winter. Before the summer was over, my pay went up to fifteen dollars a week.

My summer assignments were the customary ones for an inexperienced hand: writing obituaries and church notices; covering the police station, sheriff's office, hospitals, and funeral homes on the night shift; and checking the register at the town's three good hotels to see if any newsworthy visitors had checked in. In addition, Cannon occasionally gave me a special assignment when he had no senior reporters available.

The best of these was the coverage of a three-day convention of Panhandle cattlemen at the old Amarillo Hotel, then the cowmen's traditional hangout. A more experienced reporter covered the day sessions, dealing with such serious problems as tariffs, beef prices, and railway rates. I was responsible for whatever went on after dinner, which was mostly drinking and nostalgic talk about the old days. My observation post was, of course, the bar.

At about eight o'clock on the first evening, Col. Charles Goodnight made his entrance. That is the correct phrase. He dominated the room as soon as he stepped through the door—a big hulk of a man, not fat but broad and thick, his shoulders hunched and his head carried low like a buffalo bull. He had more presence than anyone I have ever known, except Gen. George C. Marshall. Although he was ninety-two years old that summer, he still radiated energy and moral authority.

Goodnight sat down at a table already occupied by three other elderly cattlemen. Like him, they all wore Boss of the Plains Stetsons. He ordered a toddy, bourbon whiskey with a little sugar and water. (Prohibition was still in effect, but neither the cattlemen nor their hotel seemed aware of it.) As he began to talk, I edged up to the table—timidly, for his gruffness was notorious—introduced myself, and mentioned that my mother had attended Goodnight College. To my surprise, he grinned through his Moses-style beard and said:

"I remember her. Damned fine girl. Sit down, boy, and have a toddy."

I asked for a Coke and settled in for a long night's listening. They talked of things I regarded as ancient history, if I had heard of them at all: herd drives up the Goodnight-Loving Trail . . . who really organized the posse that captured Billy the Kid at Stinking Springs . . . French Annie, one-time dance hall girl and the last inhabitant of Tascosa . . . blizzards so harsh that they drove cattle south through barbed-wire fences, or over them on heaps of frozen carcasses . . . whether John Drew actually was a cattle thief or only an incompetent ranch manager. Other old friends of Goodnight drifted by the table from time to time, till nearly everybody in the crowded bar-room had had a few words with the Colonel.* After his second toddy—and last for the evening—Goodnight began to sing cowboy songs in a cracked and wavering voice; most oldtimers within earshot joined in, but since other songs were going at distant tables he gave up after a couple of dozen verses. About midnight the old man suddenly announced that he was tired and stomped off to bed. Shortly after I went back to my office, dimly sensing that I might have witnessed something impor-tant, and spent the rest of the night writing my story. It was a poor one, too sentimental and spangled with adjectives. I wish I could have done better, because Colonel Goodnight never at-tended another cattlemen's convention; he died the following year. But I just did not know how to do justice to a living legend.

There is no need for me to try now. Good biographies of Goodnight have been written by Laura V. Hamner and J. Evetts Haley, and in one chapter of *Cow People*† Frank Dobie has explained why the Colonel "made a deeper imprint on the Great Plains than any other man who has lived there." I am concerned here mainly with one aspect of his life—how he started a flow of British money that nourished the first tenuous sprouts of civilization on the High Plains.

The necessary background can be sketched quickly. Good-night arrived in Texas in 1845, at the age of nine, when his family moved from Illinois. By the time he was twenty he and a partner were running a herd of four hundred cattle. During the Civil War he served as a scout and ranger, fighting off In-dians who thought the moment opportune for launching bloody raids all along what was then the northwest frontier of Texas. While traveling many hundreds of miles on horseback, he acquired an unsurpassable knowledge of the Plains country from the Rockies to the Arkansas border. Though he never

* A courtesy title; he never held any military rank.
† Boston: Little, Brown, 1964.

carried a map or compass, he was never lost. On one of the two occasions that I talked to him after the convention, he remarked that if he were dropped blindfolded at any spot in Texas he could tell where he was "pretty accurately" just by scanning the landscape. He had an almost miraculous talent for finding water, by watching the movement of animals and birds, by noting tracks and the contour of the land, and by some instinct that he could never explain.

Such prairie smartness enabled Goodnight to establish the three cattle trails that bore his name, the best routes leading from the Texas range land to markets in New Mexico, Colorado, Wyoming, and Kansas. Subsequently these trails were followed by hundreds of herds, wearing every brand in the book. Goodnight operated successful ranches in central Texas, New Mexico, and Colorado. And in 1875, when the Indians were cleared off the High Plains, he determined to move there, because he thought it the best cow country he had ever seen.

A Mexican mustanger, whose profession was catching and taming wild horses, had told Goodnight of a place that seemed perfect for ranching, a canyon he called the Palo Duro. It is the only thing of its kind in the High Plains, a gash nearly a thousand feet deep and sixty miles long slicing through the otherwise unbroken prairie. It was cut by the Prairie Dog Town Fork of the Red River, beginning about where the town of Canyon stands today and meandering southeastward. In width the canyon varies from a few hundred yards to fifteen miles; in effect it is a vast natural corral, since a hoofed animal can climb its clifflike sides in only a few places. (They are difficult even for a man on foot, not only because they are so steep but because their crevices are infested with rattlesnakes. When I was a boy, E. B. Fincher and I killed ten of them there in a single afternoon.) The canyon had long been a hunting ground, winter campsite, and military stronghold of the Comanches. Consequently, few white men had ever seen it, and survived, between the time Coronado's party stopped there in 1541 and

September 27, 1874, when Colonel Ranald S. MacKenzie's cavalry fought a decisive battle there in the final campaign to open up the country to white settlement.

For Goodnight's purposes, the Palo Duro offered everything. It had enough grass and water for thousands of cattle. Beneath its rimrock they would be sheltered from winter blizzards. What little fencing might be needed could be built from the trees—cedar, chinaberry, and cottonwood—that grew along the stream. Even the cow hands could enjoy the luxury of wooden bunkhouses and wood fires. All Goodnight had to do was drive out a few thousand buffalo and bring in his own cattle from Colorado. This he did in the spring of 1876. He found an old Comanche trail where the cows could descend single file, but he had to dismantle his wagons at the top of the cliff and bring their parts and all the supplies down on muleback. He set his hands to work immediately to put up horse corrals and a two-room log cabin, the first ranch house on the High Plains. His nearest neighbor was Fort Elliott, a hundred miles to the northeast.

The one thing Goodnight lacked for the ranch he envisaged—he hoped it would be the best on the continent—was money. He would need a lot of it, to stock his pastures, buy purebred bulls to improve his herd, build line camps, and eventually to buy the land he had just settled. For the time being he could graze it for nothing, but the legal ownership rested mostly with the state of Texas or with railroad companies, which had been granted large tracts as an inducement to build their lines westward. Some already had passed into the hands of Gunter, Munson and Summerfield, a firm of land speculators and surveyors. Goodnight knew it would soon be sold to other cattlemen or farmers, unless he bought it first. Trouble was that, while he owned a good many cattle and horses, he had little cash.

He thought he knew where he could get some. Among his cowboys at this time were two prosperous young men from

Great Britain who had come west primarily to see the country, hunt buffalo, and find a little adventure. One was J. C. Johnson, a Scot who later became a director of the Matador Land and Cattle Company of Dundee. The other was James T. Hughes, whose father had written a bestseller, *Tom Brown's School Days*. In all likelihood they told him about a third Britisher, John Adair, who owned a large estate in Ireland and ran a brokerage and money-lending business in Denver. In any case, Goodnight left the Palo Duro soon after his outfit was installed and headed for Denver, where he met Adair.

The two soon struck a deal—a highly advantageous one for Adair. He put up the money to buy the Palo Duro land and more cattle. Goodnight contributed his present herd to the partnership, and agreed to manage the ranch for five years at an annual salary of $2,500. Adair's investment was to be repaid in full, at 10 percent interest, and at the end of five years land and cattle were to be divided, one-third to Goodnight, the rest to Adair. Later Goodnight was to defend this reckless bargain on grounds that he was in a hurry, and could not get the money anywhere else. The truth is that he was never a clever businessman, or much interested in money for its own sake. What he really wanted was to build up the finest ranch anyone had ever seen, regardless of who got the profits.

Bigger ranches have been assembled since then, but I have never heard of a cattleman who claimed he ran a better spread than Goodnight's. At its peak, the JA covered some 1.3 million acres, either owned by the partnership or under lease. By importing Durham and Hereford stock, Goodnight bred up his herd to the highest quality yet seen in Texas. At times it numbered up to a hundred thousand head, worked by more than a hundred cowboys. Goodnight hired the best hands he could find, and then trained them further by his own rigorous standards. Among his rules were no liquor and no gambling. Any man who satisfied him for a few years could then get a foreman's job almost anywhere, being regarded as a Ph.D. in Cowmanship. The colonel also insisted on the best horses, best cooks, and best gear. To this day you will sometimes hear a particularly stout and true-lined fence referred to in the Panhandle as "a Goodnight fence."

For Adair, the venture was highly profitable. He not only got back all his capital, plus 10 percent interest (indeed, in the first five years the partnership cleared a profit of more than $500,000), but when it was finally dissolved in 1887, two years after Adair's death, his estate got control of half a million acres, stocked with prime cattle. Goodnight had bought land at prices ranging from 25 to 75 cents an acre. Today it is worth well over a hundred times that, and the ranch is still reputed to be one of the best moneymakers in the West.

Adair, who was never afflicted with modesty, let his British friends know he was on to a good thing. Other British investors, usually organized into joint stock companies, began to compete for High Plains land. Among them were the Cunard family, which put up $225,000 to start the Francklyn Land and Cattle Company; its investment in the Bar X and Diamond F brands eventually ran above a million dollars. The Earl of Aberdeen, James Charles Hamilton Gordon, and Baron Tweedmouth, Edward Marjoribanks, founded the Rocking Chair Ranche Company with offices at 25 Piccadilly, London. Its field headquarters grew into the little town of Aberdeen, where my uncle saw that bloodless gun battle. Rich linen manufacturers of Dundee backed the Matador Cattle Company, managed for fifty years by a formidable Scot named Murdo McKenzie. Three Englishmen, the Rowe brothers, headquartered their RO brand on the Salt Fork, not far from the Caperton place. Their manager, Joe Williams, often rode over to see the Caperton girls.

"I loved them all," he told me when he was an old man. "But since I could only marry one, I settled for Evelyn."

At the time of their marriage in 1899 he was the youngest manager in the Panhandle, and was accounted one of the best.

He supervised the building of 110 miles of barbed-wire fence to enclose the RO land.

Many other British-owned ranches were established, but only a few of them—notably the JA, the Matador, and the RO—were outstanding successes. Some of the other investors got out with most of their capital, but some—among them the Rocking Chair and Francklyn people—lost fortunes.

The reasons for failure were the classic ones—absentee ownership and misunderstanding. Often the British thought they were buying a remote country estate, where they could take friends from time to time to shoot buffalo, as they shot grouse in Scotland, (and a place to send feckless younger sons who were an expensive nuisance at home). Because they did not understand the Western character, the investors often picked incompetent or dishonest managers; and because they exercised only intermittent supervision, they usually discovered the mistake too late. Worse yet, when they did visit their properties, they were likely to antagonize everybody they met. In all innocence and good will, they treated cow hands with the condescension they were used to conferring on Irish peasants or Scottish crofters. They expected not only comforts unavailable in cow camps, but the kind of deference proffered by their Victorian servants at home.

This did not sit well with cowboys, who considered themselves as good as anybody, if not a damn sight better. Even Adair, who knew more about the West than most British investors, was heartily disliked by his JA employees. Goodnight described him to me as "an overbearing son of a bitch," and regretted that he had not "beat the hell out of him" on several occasions.

One night Leigh Dyer, the JA foreman, got furious over what he took to be an insult. The way I heard it, at second hand and decades after the event, was that Adair refused to eat at the same table with Dyer, when he came into ranch headquarters dusty and bloody from a long day's work castrating bull calves. After brooding for a few hours, Dyer saddled a horse, coiled a rope, and lassoed the peak of the conical, British-made tent where Adair was sleeping, leaving the poor gentleman shivering in his silk nightshirt. Goodnight fired Dyer the next day, but hired him back as soon as Adair had left the ranch. This tale my mother heard from Dyer himself, who once was one of her favorite beaus; she named my brother after him.

Goodnight, who insisted that all his hands be as bigotedly honest as he was, protected his partner against more serious retaliation. But John Drew, manager of the Rocking Chair, did not—or could not— protect its owners. On one of their rare visits, Lord and Lady Aberdeen made the mistake of calling the punchers "cow servants," and referred to tenant farmers as "cottagers." The lord expected to have his luggage carried to and from his buckboard; when the cowboys refused, Lady Aberdeen had to carry the bags herself. He also left his boots standing outside his door at ranch headquarters, and was astonished when he found them still unpolished next morning.

Small things. But cultural conflict often grows out of a string of trivialities. Then, too, hands earning thirty dollars a month for the hardest kind of labor may well have envied these uncallused foreigners who could afford to pour apparently endless sums into a business they knew nothing about. At any rate, cowboys and settlers who never would have dreamed of stealing from their neighbors came to believe it was all right to put their brands on Rocking Chair calves. I don't know that the Capertons ever did, but they undoubtedly bought some cheap beef from punchers who had suddenly acquired herds of their own.

Other ranchers, including Goodnight, believed that Drew himself mavericked calves from his employers. If so, he did it under the nose of the Honorable Archibald John Marjoribanks, brother of one of the proprietors, who had been sent out to keep books and protect the firm's interest. Evidently he never had a clue to what actually was going on. When the "ranche" was finally sold, a dozen years after its beginning, the pastures held only three hundred cattle, although the Honorable Archie's books showed fourteen thousand. It was incorporated into the neighboring Mill Iron ranch, American owned.

Such scandalous doings never afflicted British owners who settled down on their property and learned the cow business, as McKenzie and the Rowes did. But even the absentees who got robbed contributed substantially to the rapid economic growth of the country. Unwittingly, they set many a poor cowboy up in business for himself—a kind of involuntary foreign aid program.

London was then the financial capital of the world. If a flow of investment from London had not been stimulated by the Goodnight-Adair partnership, ranching would probably not have developed on the large scale for which the High Plains are uniquely suited—at least not for many years, since at the time equivalent American capital was not available.

Indirectly, the British money helped finance the country's first cultural institutions, such as courts and schools. The Collingsworth County settlers, for instance, could never have financed a county government and school system without the taxes collected from the Rocking Chair. Another example is Goodnight College, the first establishment for higher education in the Texas Panhandle (more about it in a later chapter). Although he had no children of his own, the Colonel raised the money for it from his own pocket—that is, JA profits—and from neighboring ranchers. He felt that such a civilizing influence was urgently needed, especially by the children of new settlers such as the Capertons. Mary Helen Caperton, with her passion for education, may well have had some influence on him; she knew him well. He also was moved by the fact that he had never had any formal education after the age of nine.

A brief epilogue on Colonel Goodnight. Soon after he dissolved his partnership with the Adairs, he sold his share of the

JA land and cattle and embarked on a mining venture in Mexico. It was a financial disaster. He then settled down for his final years on a relatively small ranch of his own, on the northern rim of the Palo Duro canyon. For the first time in his life he built a fairly comfortable home, far from pretentious but roomy and well furnished. It even had a second-story porch, screened from the wind on three sides, where he could sit of an evening with his toddy and watch the cattle in the canyon below.

The ranch and the college, which he started in the little town of Goodnight near his headquarters, did not begin to absorb all his energy. He collected a herd of buffalo, partly to save them from extinction, partly for a genetic experiment. By crossing them with Herefords, he hoped to get a new animal with a buffalo's stamina and the docility of a domestic cow. His "cattalo," as he called them, were not a success—the offspring of the first crosses did not reproduce themselves consistently—but his idea was a sound one. Indeed, within the last decade a California rancher, Bud Basolo, has succeeded in producing fertile hybrids, combining buffalo, Hereford, and Charolais bloodlines. I have never seen one, but have read reports that they are hardy, fatten quickly with little or no grain, and produce tender, tasty meat. In 1974 Basolo sold one of his prize bulls to a Canadian livestock breeding consortium for $2.5 million—the highest price, so far as I can discover, ever paid for a farm animal. The news would have given Colonel Goodnight a lot of satisfaction.

His wife, Mary Ann—the older sister of Leigh Dyer, his sometime foreman—died when he was ninety years old. For months he was inconsolable, and for the first time his health began to fail. Even his favorite tonic, beef extract and whiskey, did him little good. Then a letter arrived from a telegraph operator in Montana named Corinne Goodnight; she had seen his name in a newspaper story and wrote to inquire whether they might be remote relatives. As their correspondence developed, they both concluded that there probably was some such connection. On her way to vacation in Florida, Corinne stopped off to visit her pen friend. Finding him in need of nursing, she decided to stay on—for a few days, she thought—to take care of him. His health recovered miraculously, and Corinne soon become a permanent member of his household, cooking, housekeeping, and helping with his correspondence. At the age of ninety-one, he married her. She was twenty-six.

The following year—the same year I met him at the cattlemen's convention—Goodnight and his new wife visited Frank Dobie in Austin. Corinne told Dobie that she had recently had a miscarriage.

He died December 12, 1929, while he and his wife were vacationing in Phoenix, Arizona. His last full meal was of buffalo meat, sent to him from his own herd.

FIVE

Legends: Here Today and Gone Today, Too

Charles Goodnight wasted little time in conversation—he never spoke a word at table—and what he did say was memorably profane. My uncle, Joe L. Williams, on the other hand, talked whenever he could find an audience, and I never heard him utter a swearword, except as a direct quotation when he was telling a story. Nearly everything that happened to him during a long and eventful life struck him as funny. He made and lost at least three modest fortunes in the cattle business, wheat farming, land speculation, and oil, and in all these ventures he had a hilariously good time. Practically immune to worry, he would risk every penny he owned as light-heartedly as he risked his own neck. How he survived the shift from horses to automobiles baffled his family, because Joe never quite believed that there was any essential difference between them. While driving he often took both hands off the wheel for some gesture essential to his conversation. Since a horse could make its own way, why shouldn't a car?

His first car was a red Franklin with an air-cooled engine and a wickerwork body, something like an Irish jaunting cart. Passengers entered the back seat through a gate in the rear, if they could find room among the ropes, crowbars, shovels, tow chains, saddles, samples of crude oil, drilling bits, and other gear Joe habitually carried. The places Joe wanted to go, to inspect a pasture or a geological formation that hinted of oil, seldom were on roads, so he was equipped for travel over any terrain.

One day he came to Little Blue Creek at a place he thought fordable, only to find it roaring from bank to bank with a flash flood, the result of a brief cloudburst somewhere upstream. Joe knew the flood would pass in an hour or so, but as usual he was in a hurry. He drove along the creek till he found a spot where the bank on his side was about eight feet higher than the bank opposite. Then he backed away from the stream for about half a mile, lined his sights on that high bank, and pushed the hand throttle to its highest stop. The Franklin took off at about fifty miles an hour and cleared the creek as handily—Joe claimed— as any good cow pony. When it landed, though, it broke two springs and blew out a tire. Joe fixed them on the spot and went on his way. Soon afterwards, however, he traded the car in on a Buick, which he hoped would be sturdier.

When my Aunt Evelyn heard about this exploit, she decided Joe needed a driver. She nominated me, in confidence that I did not have enough nerve to jump creeks. Joe was glad to have a captive audience, even a sixteen-year-old one, and I was eager to see the country. That summer we quartered the Texas and Oklahoma Panhandles pretty thoroughly, from the Cimarron to Matador, Glenrio to Childress. Often we were on the road for a week at a time, sleeping on ranches or at forlorn country hotels. The latter Joe avoided, except when he had to do a lot of telephoning in the evening about the cattle or oil leases he had been looking at. He flirted innocently and enthusiastically with all the telephone operators—Liquid Eyes at Dalhart and Honeybunch at Texhoma were two of his favorites—and they always gave his long-distance calls priority. Like the summer with Mr. Baxter, this one turned out to be educational. I have been blessed with learned uncles.

Joe taught me how to guess, close enough, the weight of a two-year-old steer, the number of bushels per acre a field of standing wheat might yield, and how to recognize an anticline, a hump or fold in sedimentary rock strata where oil and gas sometimes accumulate. But mostly he told me stories, each of which had a moral. He urged me to pay special attention to the one about Henry Quiller because, Joe said, "it taught me how to get rich, and how never to worry about money."

"Henry was one of my hands when I was foreman of the RO," he said. "He came from a big family, and a poor one, in the Concho River country. On his eighteenth birthday his father told him it was time for him to get moving.

" 'You'll never have much chance here,' his father said. 'On this land and in this drought it's all I can do to feed your mother and the young ones. The best I can do for you is to give you part of the sheep herd. They'll starve anyway if we keep them here. I've heard there's plenty of fresh grass up north, where the country hasn't been much settled yet. So you take two hundred head and line out that way. When you come to a likely piece of land with nobody on it, file your claim.'

"Henry kissed his mother good-bye, tied a sack of beans behind his saddle, and started chaperoning those sheep. He grazed them along easy, a few miles a day. It was early in the year, the weather wasn't too hot, and he sort of enjoyed himself until his beans-and-mutton diet began to get monotonous.

"About that time, though, he came across a Mexican family living in a sod shack way off by itself in the middle of the prairie. They were trying to make a go of farming, and first off they had planted a little garden with chilies and tomatoes and such truck, as Mexicans usually do. The sight made Henry's mouth water. He offered to work a few days, setting fence posts and stringing wire, in return for all the vegetables he could eat. The Monteros were glad to have him—they needed help and company, too—so he got along fine. When the time came for Henry to move on, the old man said he wanted to give him a present.

"A couple of years earlier the Montero kids had found a stray lamb. They had named him Santa Anna and raised him as a pet. In the beginning he had been mighty cute, but now he had grown into a full-sized ram, and a mean one. He would hide around the corner of the shack until Doña Anita came out the door with an armload of laundry or something, and then he would butt her clear across the yard. He butted all the rest, too, whenever he could catch them with their backs turned. Old man Montero wanted to butcher him, but the kids wouldn't hear of it. So would Henry please take Santa Anna along with his herd?

"Henry would. He had a few rams already—nice, gentle ones—but he thought his ewes might be grateful for some more rambunctious companionship. At his age he thought he could handle anything, and he headed north again without a care in the world.

"Next evening when he was picking up buffalo chips to make a cookfire, that ram got him. For a minute Henry thought he had been hit by a locomotive, and he couldn't sit his saddle with any comfort for two days.

"From then on he tried to keep an eye on Santa Anna, but the ram was just as smart and treacherous as his namesake. He got in a couple more good licks in Henry's absent-minded moments, and a certain coolness began to grow up between them.

"By this time Henry had been traveling for nearly three months, and he had reached a country unlike anything he had ever seen. It was flat and empty and the buffalo grass was thick and nourishing. He was beginning to look for a spring or year-round creek where he could build a homestead, when he came to a canyon a mile wide and looking nearly half that deep. It was the Palo Duro, but of course Henry didn't know that at the time. Neither did he know that Charlie Goodnight had already claimed it a year earlier. All he knew was that he had found a sight he had never dreamed of—miles and miles of red cliffs with cedars growing on the slopes below and a pretty stream winding along the bottom.

"He sat down in the shade of a mesquite bush right on the cap rock, and tried to figure out some way to get his sheep down into that canyon without breaking their necks. The shade and the scenery were mighty comfortable, and pretty soon Henry remembered another present the Monteros had given him, a bundle of old newspapers. He had stuffed them in his saddlebag and forgotten about them—Henry never was much of a reader—but now they came to mind he thought he might as well find out what had happened in the world since he had left home.

"At first he couldn't find anything of much interest—some wars going on in Europe, a big fire in Chicago, a steamboat collision on the Mississippi. Then he found a page of livestock quotations, and he began to get excited. Cattle and sheep had both been going up—fast—on the Kansas City market. Henry fished out a stub of pencil and began to do some arithmetic on the edge of the paper. He calculated the present value of his herd. Then he figured what the natural increase might be each year, especially if he could shelter his sheep in that deep canyon and keep the coyotes away from the lambs. Gradually it dawned on him that he was a poor boy no longer. Already he was well off—and if the livestock market kept rising for a few more years, he could count himself a wealthy man.

"He looked at his woolies, grazing peacefully in that good grass, with a new affection. And then he saw Santa Anna at the edge of the herd, pawing the ground with his head down and getting bunched up for a charge.

" 'Let him come,' Henry said to himself. 'A rich man like me doesn't have to put up with that damned old outlaw any longer.'

"He stood there, with his back to the canyon, and held out his newspaper at arm's length, like a bullfighter's cape, to give the ram a good target. Santa Anna aimed right at it, with a full head of steam.

"What Henry hadn't figured was that the rest of the herd had got in the habit of following Santa Anna. When the ram lunged through that newspaper and took off the cliff, the whole herd was strung out behind him, running hell for leather.

" 'There wasn't much I could do,' Henry explained when he told the story years later, 'except to start grabbing with both hands. One minute I was practically a rich man. The next minute I didn't have a thing in the world but nine pounds of wool and seven sheep tails.

" 'Right then I realized that wealth was a snare and an illusion, and from that day on I've never tried to make a lot of money. I knew I could never hold onto it if I got it.' "

Like Joe Williams himself, I've kept Henry's theory of economics in mind ever since.

Another of Joe's cautionary tales concerned Apple Axe, who once poured whiskey and helped the cook at the Equity Bar in Tascosa. Nobody now remembers how he got his nickname, or what his last name was. When I saw his grave on Tascosa's Boot Hill a couple of years ago, the inscription on his marker just read "Apple Axe."

"For a while there," Joe told me, "Tascosa was a little rough. It was the only place in nearly a hundred miles where cowboys could go to gamble and drink on payday. Naturally some hard characters collected there—cardsharps and mule freighters, and sometimes Billy the Kid and his outlaws would ride in from New Mexico. Old Apple tried to keep things nice and peaceful with his bung starter, but now and then the unruly element got too many for him. In one of those intemperate Saturday night discussions he lost an eye.

"A few weeks later some of the customers began to complain. They said they didn't like that empty socket staring at them across the bar. Claimed it made them kind of nervous and morose and interfered with their drinking. So Apple, who always tried to please, wrote off to Sears, Roebuck in Chicago and ordered a glass eye.

"At first the Equity regulars applauded and told Apple how handsome he looked. But before long they were complaining again. Because he didn't want to be discourteous, Old Apple always drank along with his customers, glass for glass. As a result, along about two o'clock in the morning his good eye would get pretty bloodshot. His glass eye, of course, did not keep step. So there he would be, leaning on the bar with a shot glass in his hand, with one eye red and the other as white as a hen's egg. Some of the more sensitive cowboys found this disconcerting, and told him so.

"Apple wrote off to Sears, Roebuck again to order a bloodshot glass eye. It didn't arrive for months, because it was a special order, and expensive to boot. But when he got it, Apple put his strategy into operation right away. He would keep a close watch on his good eye in the bar mirror, and as soon as he noticed it turning red, he would swap his regular glass eye for the special bloodshot number. This nightly exchange bothered some of the boys, and they insisted that he squat down out of sight behind the bar while he was doing it.

"Even so, his customer relations were not altogether satisfactory. The bloodshot glass eye, it turned out, was a little smaller than the regular one. So in the course of a busy evening, it would roll in the socket. Sometimes it would stare at the ceiling and sometimes at the floor, while Apple's good eye would be looking straight at you. More complaints.

"In a last desperate effort to make everybody happy, Apple

tried to pack that wandering eye into firm place with a wad of cotton. Trouble this time was that some of the cotton would work out, making a kind of white fringe all around that red eyeball. The public consensus was that this made Old Apple look more hideous than ever, and trade began to fall off. Jack Ryan, who owned the Equity, finally had to let him go.

"Somebody shot Apple Axe eventually, but I don't think it was on account of the eye. I heard there was a misunderstanding about something else."

After pondering that story for a few miles, I told Joe I was sure it had a moral, but I couldn't see what it was.

"Plain enough," he said. "Don't ever try to look better than God made you. You don't fool anybody, and you do yourself no good."

Joe never tried to be anything but his natural self. Several times in his career he could easily have afforded a fancy office and a swarm of secretaries. He preferred to operate out of his car and a spare bedroom in his Amarillo home, where he installed an old desk and two filing cabinets. Most of his letters he typed out himself, though he dictated contracts and complicated documents to a stenographer in his lawyer's office. Once he became a businessman, he never affected the cowboy costume with boots and a big hat that is so dear to many Texas bankers, shoe salesmen, and used car dealers. Joe settled for an ordinary, rumpled business suit and a bow tie.

Evelyn and her sisters made a powerful and sustained effort to reform Joe, but they never budged him an inch. For nearly fifty years they failed to inspire him toward any of the finer things, such as church going, edifying literature, serious music, and the modest social life that Amarillo offered. But Joe, like a number of cowboys, was remarkably well read, thanks to Arbuckle's Coffee. This was a favorite brand in cow camps. It was high roast, strong, and laced with chicory; but its main attraction was the Little Blue Books. These were editions of the classics, published by Haldeman-Julius in Kansas City and retailed at a nickel. All had blue paper covers, measured three inches square, and ran to about fifty pages—enough for one of Shakespeare's plays, in small type, or a selection of Longfellow's poems, or an excerpt from Dickens. (Haldeman-Julius never touched anything under copyright, because they did not like to pay author's royalties.) Since one of these books fitted neatly into a coffee can, Arbuckle bought up the overstock and enclosed them with his product. They proved to be a highly successful merchandising premium, at least in the West. A cowboy could tuck several Little Blue Books into a pocket, handy for reading in the saddle during quiet moments on herd duty—the best available remedy for boredom. When he finished one, he would trade it for a different title, until the books fell apart. Today, I understand, they are collectors' items, because few survived. While they lasted, they were a major cultural influence on the plains; Joe Williams had read reams of the world's best literature before he was twenty-five. Perhaps because of his Welsh parentage, he was especially fond of poetry, and could recite Fitz-Greene Halleck by the yard. But Evelyn never could interest him in the novels of Harold Bell Wright or tracts of Methodist evangelists. In the little leisure he allowed himself, he preferred to reread Poe or Mark Twain. Or to listen to "Amos 'n' Andy" on the radio; I don't think he missed a program as long as they were on the air.

Her failure to modernize Joe's literary tastes grieved Evelyn, but not so much as her failure to wean him away from whiskey. For family reasons noted earlier, all the Caperton women were dead set against liquor of any kind, in any quantity. All Joe ever took was a nip before lunch and before dinner, but Evelyn's considerable eloquence—and her sisters'—never persuaded him to give up that small comfort. All through prohibition he kept a half-gallon jar of bootleg corn in his filing cabinet, and he carried a pint when he was on the road. In all our travels, however, he never offered me a drink—believing, I suppose, that he should not tempt a growing boy into bad habits.

Because he was fanatically loyal to his friends, Joe never told anybody where he got his whiskey until after prohibition was repealed. Then, when indiscretion could do no harm, he disclosed his source. An elderly farmer named Pop Fleener had run a still in his barn near Plumb Nelly—so called, Joe said, because it was "plumb out yander and nelly to Colorado." He was an honest craftsman who turned out a superior product, fermented from corn, bran, and sugar mash and processed through a real copper still. Some of his competitors were less scrupulous. The cheapest and most deadly liquor of that time was horse-blanket whiskey. Its makers threw into the mash anything that was handy—potato peelings, leftover oatmeal, cotton-seed cake, molasses, for example. And instead of investing in a proper still, they simply heated the mash in a galvanized iron washtub, with a horse blanket thrown over it. When the blanket was saturated with alcohol-laden fumes, they ran it through a clothes wringer and bottled the runoff. One consumer of such moonshine claimed, shortly before he died of delirium tremens, that he could tell whether the blanket had belonged to a quarter horse or a Morgan. At least, that's the way Joe told it.

Early in his career Pop Fleener had been arrested twice by deputy sheriffs while he was delivering his produce. Since he found the county jail uncomfortable and the company boring, he resolved never again to take a chance on selling and transporting. Manufacturing was safe enough, since his barn was never raided. From then on, all he sold was maps. As soon as he ran off a batch, he decanted it into half-gallon jars. These he buried at night in caches scattered around the countryside for a radius of twenty miles, some in the ditch beside a country road, others in a clump of shinnery oak or in a corner of a remote pasture. Each time he planted a deposit of whiskey, he made a detailed map of its location, with a note on the quantity. You could buy a half-gallon map for two dollars or a five-gallon map for twenty, with comparable prices for any amount in between. Then you could dig up your liquor whenever you liked—and if you got caught on the way home, that was your tough luck, not Pop's.

Joe was never afraid of getting caught because he knew all the deputy sheriffs, and some of them had worked for him on the RO ranch; but I think he enjoyed the whiff of conspiracy that went with the maps and the nocturnal digging. I was glad when he finally told me about these arrangements. Until then I had never understood why he always carried a spade in the back of his car.

SIX

The Misleading History
of Old Tascosa

Throughout its brief life, Tascosa misled people: the cowboys who went there looking for romance and glamour, the Spanish-Americans who hoped to establish a pastoral idyll, the few wives who tried to make it an outpost of civilization, the tradesmen who thought it would become the metropolis of the High Plains, and the land speculators who believed it would make them rich. Long after its death it has continued to mislead millions of people, through countless Western novels, films, and television shows. For Tascosa—along with a very few other places such as Dodge City and Abilene—became the fictional prototype of the frontier Western town, the mythical setting of a thousand gunfights.

In fact, Tascosa was anything but typical. The representative settlements were towns like Childress, Shamrock, Clarendon, and scores of others where nothing much ever happened and gunsmoke was as rare as oysters. Nobody ever heard of them—

while Tascosa became an enduring legend, because for a few years it did have more than its share of excitement and bloodshed. But it was never a romantic or glamorous place. It was a sordid, grubby little village, and most of its residents led hard, sad, and disappointed lives.

Like most towns, Tascosa grew up where two trails intersected. One of them was the old Indian trace, also known as the Spanish Road, that followed the Canadian River from west to east across the Texas Panhandle. The other was a track the buffalo followed in their annual northern and southern migrations. At what eventually became the site of Tascosa they had found an easy place to cross the river. Its banks were low, the stream was wide, shallow, and relatively free of quicksand, and several creeks converged there from the north. Beside these creeks and on the flood plain of the Canadian was a lush growth of river grass, quite different from the short grass of the prairie. It grew as high as a buffalo's belly and stayed green most of the year—a rare treat for any grazing animal. The Comanches, following the buffalo, often camped there for a week or more to rest and fatten their horses. The Spanish explorers used the same crossing, and later so did the wagon freighters and cattlemen trailing their herds north to market.

The first settlers there probably were Mexican *comancheros,* who carried on a profitable business with the Indians, trading guns, ammunition, knives, and cloth for the cattle and horses the Comanches had stolen. Before 1875 these traders were the only non-Indians who could venture onto the High Plains in relative safety. Even they were occasionally pillaged and scalped by a band of whimsical raiders, but most of the time the Comanches kept their tacit truce. By 1874, or a few years earlier, several Mexican families had felt secure enough to build adobe homes near the crossing of the Canadian.* Their settle-

* These, alas, did not turn out to be permanent habitations; so Colonel Goodnight's cabin in the Palo Duro holds title to being the first permanent homestead on the High Plains.

ment was called Plazito Borregos, after the Borregos family, which had led a group of land-hungry immigrants from Taos.

To the eyes of the Mexicans, this spot was a near paradise. By cultural traditions handed down from both Spaniards and Indians, they were gardeners and shepherds—unlike the American cattlemen, who loathed any work that could not be done on horseback. Here was one of the few places on the High Plains where it was possible to raise fruit and vegetables, as the Alibates people had discovered thousands of years earlier. Wild turkey, antelope, bears, and elk were abundant. For the settlers' flocks of sheep and goats there was luxuriant pasture, sheltered from winter blizzards by the creek banks. One of these spring-fed streams had been dammed by beaver; the Borregos clan called it Atascosa, which means "boggy."

The first Lucifer to trouble this pastoral heaven was Sostenes l'Archeveque, a thief and murderer without any known trace of redeeming social value. He probably killed more men than Billy the Kid—legend puts the score as high as twenty-three—but he was never romanticized into a Robin Hood character as Billy was. In the summer of 1876 he made the mistake of murdering two brothers from California, named Casner, who were trailing a herd of sheep toward the Palo Duro country. They had a horde of twenty-dollar gold pieces, some of which Sostenes found at their last camp.*

At this time the *alcade,* or head man, of the Borregos settlement was Colas Martinez, a prosperous sheep man who happened to be Sostenes' brother-in-law. Martinez was also a friend of Goodnight's, and had in fact encouraged him to take his cattle to the Palo Duro rather than settle in the Canadian valley, which the Mexicans already had preempted. Colas had also promised Goodnight—a fanatic about law and order—that he would see to it that Sostenes did not steal any Goodnight livestock, or otherwise misbehave beyond toleration.

---

* According to oral tradition, he did not get an additional $20,000 that they had hidden somewhere along the trail. Cow hands are still looking for it.

Martinez was as good as his word. He knew that the murder of the Casner brothers meant trouble for the whole Mexican community. Consequently he arranged, in council with the other settlers, to have the outlaw executed next time he showed up at Plazito Borregos. Shortly afterwards Sostenes did come in, to ask for food at the home of the Gurules family; the Gurules brothers stabbed him to death as he came through the door.

This act of justice did not avert further trouble, as the *alcade* had hoped. When John Casner, father of the slain men, heard about their murder he swore he would wipe out the whole Borregos community in retaliation. He set out from Silver City, New Mexico, with his remaining son and two friends, hard-bitten Texans who had no objections to killing Mexicans, guilty or innocent. In a series of treacherous attacks, the Casner party killed Colas Martinez and three of his neighbors before they were driven away, with the loss of one of the Texans. Fearing that the Casners would return, a number of Mexican families abandoned their homesteads along the Canadian and fled back to New Mexico. Thus began the tradition of violence, usually senseless, that was to haunt Tascosa from then on.

As soon as the Casner scare died down, the trickle of migration from New Mexico to the Canadian valley resumed. Nearly all of the newcomers were peaceable, hard-working families with many children. Some of them, like Casimero Romero, were wealthy Castilians; he arrived in a luxurious (that is, well-sprung and upholstered) coach, followed by fourteen prairie schooners and a troop of relatives and retainers. They built adobe homes north of the river, opposite Plazito Borregos, and from about that time in the winter of 1876 the little settlement began to be known as Tascosa. It had already acquired a few Anglo-American residents, the first of whom was Henry Kimball, who had seen the valley when he was serving in the army and had fallen in love with it. As soon as his enlistment expired, he moved there and set up a blacksmith shop in a one-room adobe hut. Soon after G. J. Howard and Ira Rinehart started the town's second business establishment, a general store selling flour, bacon, blankets, ammunition, patent medicines, whiskey, and a few other necessities. It opened at an auspicious moment, just before the arrival of the Romero clan virtually doubled the town's population.

The real boom started with the coming of the cattlemen. The first of these was Thomas S. Bugbee, a veteran of the Union army and a former street-car conductor in Washington, D.C., who established the Quarter Circle T ranch on a tributary of the Canadian to the east of Tascosa in 1876. A little later Ellsworth Torrey, who may have been a retired British naval officer, settled west of Tascosa. He had the backing of a Boston bank, so he was able to build a comparatively comfortable home for his wife and four children, and within a few years built up a herd of perhaps twenty-five thousand cattle. But the Torreys did not stay long. According to some accounts, Mrs. Torrey could not stand the loneliness; according to others, Ellsworth had trouble with Billy the Kid's band of outlaws. At any rate, they sold their livestock to the LS ranch and moved back east. The only reminder of them today is the Torrey Peaks, a jumble of rocky hills on what was once their range.

A third ranch was founded in 1877 when Maj. George W. Littlefield sent a herd of his LIT cattle down the trail from Dodge City. Like earlier settlers, Littlefield had no title to any land. But although it belonged to the state of Texas or the railroads, it had never been surveyed, and by long-accepted custom it could be preempted—temporarily—for grazing by anyone who found a vacant range to his liking. The LIT manager, C. S. McCarty, claimed a huge acreage east and north of Tascosa. For headquarters, he bought Henry Kimball's blacksmith shop because it had ample water nearby—both Tascosa Creek and a dependable spring. Whoever controlled water also controlled grazing land for miles around.*

Later that same year two wealthy Bostonians who were in-

*Littlefield sold the LIT in 1881 to a Scottish syndicate, the Prairie Cattle Company, one of the less successful British ventures into the cattle business.

vesting in Western ventures, D. T. Beals and W. H. Bates, started the LX ranch with headquarters about twenty miles down the river from Tascosa. To manage it, they hired a rank stranger who rode in on a gaunt horse and asked for work—a reckless decision that has never been satisfactorily explained. He gave his name as W. C. "Bill" Moore; nobody in that part of the country knew anything about him, although later rumors held that he killed at least two men elsewhere when he was wearing other identities. It was also widely believed that he put his own brand on a good many LX calves, and encouraged his cowboys to do a little mavericking of their own. Certainly he had a penchant for hiring rough characters, including Charlie Siringo, Jim East, Lee Hall, Cape Willingham, and others who were to become legendary in the history of that frontier. However dubious his honesty, Moore had a talent for leadership. His hands were unswervingly loyal to him, rather than the ranch, and some killed at his command.

Other brands running on the range near Tascosa at about that time were the LS, owned by the Lee-Scott Company, the Frying Pan, and the XIT, biggest of them all. It eventually covered some 3 million acres, given by the state to a syndicate of Chicago financiers in payment for their building of the capitol in Austin. Most of these ranches bought at least some of their supplies from Tascosa merchants, who freighted in goods by wagon train. And all of their cowboys naturally visited the town for what passed in those days as Rest and Recreation—liquor, cards, and women.

Tascosa had another attraction. It was at least a hundred miles away from the nearest peace officer. A wanted man could feel as safe there, at least from the law, as if he were in Tibet. So a good many vagrants-on-horseback drifted in, looking for work as a cow hand, monte dealer, bartender, or livery stable roustabout—or, failing that, as horse thief, cattle rustler, or stage robber, professions in which they were often experienced. Customarily they were known only by nicknames—Latigo Jim and Mexican Frank, for example. So, too, were the women who hung around the bars and entertained friends at their shanties in a Tascosa suburb known as Hogtown. A few of them are noted in the scanty records of the town as Frog Lip Sadie, Box Car Jane, Midnight Rose, Slippery Sue, Canadian Lily, and Homely Ann. The evidence suggests that they were practical rather than romantic types.

As the town grew, it also attracted more respectable residents. James E. McMasters, a Quaker from Pennsylvania, started a second store, and in 1879 Tascosa acquired its largest structure yet—the Exchange Hotel, with three bedrooms and a spacious dining hall, which also served as a ballroom on special occasions. It was run with impeccable decorum by Mr. and Mrs. H. A. Russell and their four children. The rates were fifty cents for a bed and fifty cents for a meal. Jack Ryan, a former LX wagon boss, opened the Equity Bar next door, dispensing whiskey at ten cents per glass. A less decorous hotel, with saloon and general store attached, was operated by Jack Cone in Hogtown. Murdo McKenzie, manager of the Matador ranch, was staying there one night when he was awakened by several shots. He jumped out of bed and ran into the saloon, where he saw a wounded man lying on the floor and two other men kneeling by a whiskey barrel that had been punctured by a stray bullet. McKenzie asked them if the wounded man needed help.

"Hell, yes," one of them replied, "but if we leave this barrel all the whiskey will go to waste."

By the time it reached its peak population, about 1885, Tascosa had sixty houses, including both residences and business establishments—all but one of them single-story adobes. It enjoyed such ornaments of civilization as a millinery shop, a drugstore, a surveyor's office, two restaurants, seven bars, a jewelry store, three barbers' chairs, a livery stable, and a doctor. (The latter was Dr. Henry C. Hoyt, at that time a close friend of Billy the Kid; he eventually became Surgeon General of the United States Army.) For a brief period it even had a school, where

Clayton McCrea tried to teach reading and writing to about thirty pupils, half Mexican and half American. And for five years, beginning in 1886, C. F. Rudolph published the Tascosa *Pioneer,* an enterprising and often brilliantly written weekly newspaper. Its file in the Panhandle-Plains Historical Society Museum in Canyon gives the most complete account available of daily life in Tascosa.

The issue of June 12, 1886, reported that an itinerant minister, the Reverend Bloodworth, had "preached . . . to a small but respectful congregation." This event led Rudolph to editorialize that

> society is not half so rough as many have been led to believe. . . . It is true that our social regulations have been guiltless of church or Sunday School. But in general the people of Tascosa are wholehearted, social, and exceptionally civil. Law-breaking is the exception and not the rule.

The community served not only the surrounding ranches, but also the trail herders driving cattle from the lower Panhandle and central Texas to market at the Dodge City railhead. A trail crew was usually composed of a foreman, a cook with his chuck wagon, five or six cowboys, and a horse wrangler who minded three or four extra mounts for each hand. The herd itself ordinarily numbered about fifteen hundred cattle. Their route forded the Canadian at its easy crossing and ran right through the middle of town, between the Exchange Hotel and McMasters' store, on its way north. Often a trail crew would stop for a day or two on the outskirts of Tascosa while the cattle grazed the tall river grass, the cook and foreman stocked up the wagon, and the hands patronized the bars.

Both these transients and the cowboys from the neighboring ranches were likely to be young, rambunctious, and—when they hit town for the first time in weeks—eager for action. Moreover, in the early days many of them buckled on a gun belt when they came to Tascosa. Such customers, mixed with whiskey, cards, and a short supply of women, were likely, obviously, to be somewhat explosive.

The resulting fireworks have been described in full, if not monotonous, detail by John L. McCarty in his *Maverick Town: The Story of Old Tascosa.** He began gathering material for the book in the early thirties, when both he and I worked on the Amarillo *Globe-News,* and I sometimes went with him when he was searching for old records and interviewing people who had once lived in Tascosa. I am convinced that his information is as accurate as he could make it. Consequently, when he differs in minor details from Haley, Hamner, and the other scanty sources available—including a few old-timers who told me about events as they remembered them from forty years earlier—I have generally relied on McCarty.†

Sad to say, one Tascosa gunfight was much like another, and none of them resembled the scene, so often portrayed on TV and in films, of two duelists stalking toward each other down Main Street at high noon. Unlike Gary Cooper and John Wayne, most Tascosa gunmen preferred to shoot their victims in the back, and in the dark.

A few cases did have their points of interest, such as that of Fred Leigh, an LS foreman who rode into town one day half drunk. Feeling playful, he shot the head off a duck that was paddling in a mudhole on Spring Street. This so startled a pregnant Mexican woman that she fainted. Cape Willingham, who observed these proceedings, felt he had to remonstrate; he was one of the town's most responsible citizens, who had worked for both Goodnight and the LX and had established the first mail route between Tascosa and Dodge City. Though unarmed, he chided Leigh for shooting a duck in the presence

* Norman: University of Oklahoma Press, 1946.
† For example, Frederick W. Rathjen, in his excellent history, *The Texas Panhandle Fronter* (Austin: University of Texas Press, 1973), names the Romero party as the first settlers of Tascosa, although he grants the possibility of earlier Mexican residents in the neighborhood.

of a nervous woman, and suggested that he would be more welcome if he did not carry weapons while in Tascosa. Leigh replied that he would shoot his ducks where he found them, and wear his hardware when he pleased. Willingham walked into a nearby saloon, and got a double-barreled shotgun. When he came out and repeated his request, Leigh reached for his pistol. Willingham blew him out of the saddle.

In neither Western novels nor films have I ever encountered a gunfight over a duck, nor did it happen again in Tascosa. Most killings there were just murders over money, or out of sheer meanness. For instance, a drunk cowboy went to sleep in a dance hall girl's room, and was found later with his pockets empty and a bullet hole in the back of his head. His brother suspected Johnnie Maley, a bartender; though he had no solid evidence, he walked into the saloon and shot Maley, without either inquiry or warning. Another typical case was the killing of a transient stranger known as the Dutchman by John Gough, alias the Catfish Kid. The Dutchman was making his bed on some straw in the lot behind Cone's store when the Kid stopped by, started an argument, and shot the stranger, who was unarmed. In reporting the incident in the *Pioneer*, Editor Rudolph said: "It was cold blooded murder and Catfish Kid should be dealt with. He has done enough meanness around here already."

I can find no evidence how, or whether, the Kid was ever "dealt with."

By 1880 the more respectable members of the community— and especially their wives—decided that a little law and order would be a good thing. They had considerable hopes for Tascosa, believing that it might soon outgrow its two rival settlements—Mobeetie, which had sprung up beside Fort Elliott, and Clarendon, far to the southeast—and thus become the dominant town of the High Plains. But these ambitions clearly implied some kind of government. Consequently, they organized Oldham County, with Tascosa as the county seat, Cape Willingham as sheriff, and McMasters, the Quaker merchant, as judge. A little later, needing a justice of the peace to handle minor offenses, they chose the town butcher, Alexander "Scotty" Wilson, a man of firm views. When he fined one miscreant $200 for disorderly conduct, the man protested that the penalty was excessive and that he intended to appeal to a higher court.

"Sit down, you son of a bitch," Wilson said, "Sit down, I say. There ain't no higher court."

To give substance to its new status, Tascosa put up its only stone building, a two-story courthouse and jail. Here justice was dispensed, not only for Oldham County, but for nine neighboring counties that had been designated by lines on the map of Texas but did not yet have organized governments. Today this courthouse is the only remnant of the original town—unless you count Boot Hill, the cemetery on a little knoll overlooking the Canadian. It is still fenced with barbed wire, and most of its twenty-seven graves have some kind of markers, memorializing men who died with their boots on. Citizens who died more peacefully were usually buried in another place called Cheyenne Cemetery; no trace of it remains.

Incidentally, so far as I can discover, violence in Tascosa seldom if ever had racial overtones. In general, Mexican and Anglo-American residents got along well together. The frequent dances and fiestas at the Mexican *plazitos* were the town's most popular social functions, and intermarriage between the two groups was common. Negro cowboys, who were fairly numerous, apparently were treated in both camps and barrooms on equal terms with their white companions. One of them, Matthieu "Bones" Hooks, became famous as the best horse breaker in the Panhandle, and was hired for this special chore from time to time by nearly all of the big ranches. Another, Bose Ikard, was described by Goodnight as "the most skilled and trustworthy" cowboy he ever had, "very good in a fight," and surpassing everybody else in "endurance and stamina." Goodnight added that: "I have trusted him farther than any living man." They remained devoted friends until Ikard's death in 1929, a few months before Goodnight's.

In temperament and business methods, however, the Mexicans and Anglos were significantly different. A Mexican hacienda on the High Plains was essentially a family enterprise, managed by a patriarch whose ambition was to provide a comfortable living for his relatives and retainers. Such an establishment produced nearly everything needful, from chickens to chilies, rawhide furniture to homemade saddles. It had little need for cash, and thus no reason to drive great herds to distant markets, or to control ever-increasing acreages of grass.

The successful American ranches, on the other hand, were essentially big-business enterprises, geared to produce the maximum cash return for their owners. Typically the owner was a corporation, financed with either British or Eastern capital, and operating its enterprise through a hired manager. In the early days of free grass and apparently unlimited space, some managers—such as Bill Moore—encouraged their cowboys to register brands of their own and to graze their cattle along with those of the ranch. Eventually some of the thriftier hands accumulated enough livestock to establish separate ranches. For a few years the High Plains really did seem to be a land of boundless opportunity, where any ambitious young man with a long rope could found an estate of baronial proportions.

This illusion did not last long. The big ranching corporations were quick to perceive three facts of High Plains economics:

1. The era of free grass and open range was ephemeral. Any ranch that hoped to survive would have to acquire legal title to its land as promptly as possible—as Colonel Goodnight had done in the Palo Duro. And with a few exceptions, only the corporate enterprises commanded enough capital to buy up or lease the large acreages that were necessary for profitable operations in that country.

2. The small, individually owned ranches were often

stocked—at least in part—with calves that legally should have worn the brand of one of the big ranches. Nearly every cowboy carried a running iron—a rod with a curved tip. By heating this tip over a cow-chip fire, the cowboy could trace his own brand on any unmarked animal he came across, as easily as if he were drawing it with chalk on a blackboard. If he were a little more unscrupulous, he could also superimpose his brand over one the cow already wore. Thus LS could easily be converted into T-48, a brand registered in the name of Tom Harris, a small rancher of dubious repute. Among the big ranches, only the XIT and LIT brands were known to be virtually immune to such forgeries.

3. Cattle could be raised most profitably in fenced pastures, rather than on the open range. Under fence, they could be handled by fewer men, they were less likely to drift off before storms, and they were less liable to theft. Any thief could cut a fence, of course—but if he were found with an unbranded, or misbranded, calf inside a fenced pasture, the presumption of guilt was clear, and usually fatal. The JA hands hanged a thief without legal ceremonies in the Palo Duro in 1877, and similar incidents were by no means rare in other parts of the Plains country, though they were seldom recorded.

Most significant of all, fencing made possible the improvement of the breed. So long as cattle roamed the open range, they bred at random. But when a rancher could put his cows inside a fenced pasture, drive out the longhorn bulls, and introduce a few imported Hereford or Durham sires, the quality of his calf crop would improve from year to year.

Fencing became feasible within the decade after 1874, when Joseph F. Glidden patented the first practical barbed wire. This was a technological development as important as the six-shooter and the windmill in the settlement of the High Plains. Its story, and Glidden's role in Plains history, deserve a separate chapter. The point to be noted here is that Glidden made his invention shortly before Tascosa reached its peak in population and hopes for the future; and that his invention helped doom the town to extinction.

By that time the big corporation ranchers were losing whatever enthusiasm they had ever felt for Tascosa. They coveted the access to water along its creeks and the Canadian River, which in many places was controlled by Mexican squatters or individual cattlemen. Moreover, they regarded it as a nesting ground for thieves and outlaws. In addition to the illicit branding so often practiced in the Tascosa neighborhood, Billy the Kid occasionally used it as a base for more serious depredations. He and his gang—probably never more than ten men—would drive whole herds of cattle, branded and unbranded, into New Mexico. There he sold them to an accomplice who butchered them and sold the carcasses to the army post at Fort Stanton.

Regarding the infant government of Oldham County as inadequate to stop such outlawry, the big cattlemen decided to do it themselves. In 1880 a group of them—led, not surprisingly, by Charles Goodnight—organized the Panhandle Cattlemen's Association, hired a "range detective" named Frank Stewart, and instructed him to abate the Billy the Kid gang permanently. They also offered Stewart whatever help he needed in the way of manpower, horses, food, and ammunition.

What amounted to a small military expedition was organized at Tascosa, under the direction of the LX and LIT managers. It included Charlie Siringo, who later wrote the most famous of all cowboy autobiographies, Jim East, Lee Hall, Lon Chambers, and perhaps a dozen other hands from nearby ranches. This heavily armed posse, with cooks, wagons, and extra horses, headed west on November 16, 1880, hoping to find the Kid somewhere in New Mexico. It was joined a few days later by a smaller party under command of Pat Garrett, sheriff of Lincoln County, New Mexico, who also was on the Kid's trail.

The subsequent events have been related so often, and in such detail, that they have become, in effect, a subbranch of

Western scholarship. In bare-bones summary, a long and exhausting pursuit ended in the killing of two of the Kid's gang and the capture of three others and the Kid himself in an abandoned rock house at Stinking Springs. A few months later the Kid escaped from jail, after killing two of his guards. Garrett took up the pursuit again, and finally ambushed the Kid in a bedroom of an adobe building in Fort Sumner, New Mexico. Thus ended, on July 14, 1881, the career of Tascosa's most notorious sometime resident—originally christened William Bonney, a juvenile delinquent from Brooklyn who had drifted west and reputedly killed twenty-one men before his own death at twenty-one.

This had a chilling effect on large-scale rustling, but the petty mavericking in the Canadian valley went on much as before. To combat it, the big cattlemen hired Garrett, whose efficiency as a nemesis of thieves was now well established. They arranged to have him commissioned as a temporary captain of Texas Rangers, gave him a headquarters at the LS ranch, and helped him recruit a small Ranger company, largely from among the more violent of the LS cowboys. His coming caused much resentment among the little ranchers and the Mexican nesters, who suspected—with good reason—that the Rangers were merely part of the corporations' plan to take over the whole Canadian valley for themselves. Something like class warfare developed between the "little men" and the "big men," the latter including the Rangers and the cowboys in corporation pay. A series of murders and gunfights culminated, in the spring of 1886, in what is still known throughout the Panhandle as the Big Fight. It started as a quarrel over a woman, Sally Emory, between members of the two factions—Ed King, an LS hand, and Lem Woodruff, a partisan of the nesters. Within minutes after the first shots were fired, in front of Jenkins' and Dunn's saloon, nearly all of Tascosa's Main Street was blazing with gunfire, as other members of both factions rallied around. The fight ended with Woodruff badly wounded, King and two other LS cowboys dead, and an innocent bystander, Jesse Sheets, killed by mistake. Nobody ever knew how many men took part in this confused battle; I have heard estimates, from survivors or onlookers, as high as twenty, but that probably is an exaggeration. Five men, including Woodruff, were tried for murder. All were acquitted.

The Big Fight, and the acquittals, were counted as victories of a sort for the little men. But the ranchers continued their campaign against the Tascosa community with a more decisive weapon—money. They bought up or leased the land occupied by the squatters and evicted them, one family after another, sometimes but not always paying a small sum for the buildings and corrals. Moreover, they began fencing their land. The first barbed wire in the Canadian River country was strung in 1882 by its inventor, Joseph Glidden, and his partner, Henry B. Sanborn, who had established the Frying Pan ranch on 250,000 acres southeast of Tascosa. Theirs was in part a demonstration project, since they knew if their fence proved successful they would soon be selling wire by the carload to neighboring ranchers. Consequently they built their fence so solidly that parts of it were still in use as late as 1940.

The LX, LS, LIT, and Turkey Track outfits soon followed the example of the Frying Pan, and by 1884 the XIT started work on what proved to be the biggest fencing job of all time, enclosing 3 million acres with 1,500 miles of four-strand fence.

The fencing, of course, stopped the trail herds that had brought much business to the Tascosa stores, saloons, and dance hall girls. By 1885 the town was fenced in on all sides, and the trail herds still coming up from the south had to make long detours around the town and the ranches that encapsulated it. The big outfits had also stopped buying their supplies in Tascosa, preferring to operate their own wagon trains from the nearest railheads. One by one the stores and bars closed their doors, and the townspeople began to drift away, as the squatter sheep- and cattlemen had, to other settlements. Even Casimero Romero, the *jefe* of the Spanish-speaking inhabitants, sold his herds in 1882, and after a few years of running a butcher shop and a freighting business in Tascosa, moved his family back to New Mexico.

Until almost the last issue of the Tascosa *Pioneer,* its editor held out hope that the town might yet be saved by the coming of the railroads, which were beginning to push their way into the Panhandle. Surely one of them would use the famous Tascosa crossing of the Canadian River—and if two lines happened to intersect there, the town might yet become the metropolis of the High Plains. This hope faded when the Fort Worth and Denver bridged the Canadian a few miles above Tascosa. Its tracks eventually crossed those of the Santa Fe and the Rock Island lines at Amarillo, an upstart community that was not even settled until 1887—but which was to become, thanks to the railroads, the principal city of the Panhandle and the world's biggest shipping point for cattle. Amarillo's rise naturally hastened Tascosa's decline.

The final blows were a prolonged drought, followed by a flood. From 1889 to 1891 so little rain fell on the High Plains that the Canadian dried up entirely for months at a time, and sandstorms heaped dust piles in the Tascosa streets. Then in September of 1893 a torrential three-day rain sent the Canadian booming far beyond its normal banks. The flood destroyed seventeen houses in Tascosa and damaged others so badly that repair hardly seemed worthwhile. Most of the remaining inhabitants gave up at this point, leaving the town with little but its courthouse, one store, one saloon, a few girls, and a scattered handful of nesters.

The end came, for all practical purposes, in 1915, when the county seat was moved to Vega and the courthouse emptied of its records. The stone building was taken over as headquarters for the LIT ranch, which had passed from the ownership of the Prairie Cattle Company of Dundee to Lee Bivins of Amarillo. The last remaining family, so far as I can determine, was that of Al Morris, who raised apples on what had been the Romero homestead. In the twenties he and his sons tore down the crumbling adobe walls that survived in the Hogtown quarter and planted the ground to squash.

One lone inhabitant outlasted even the Morrises. Frenchy was a dance hall girl who had run away from a convent in Louisiana and had drifted to Tascosa in its early days by way of Dodge City and Mobeetie. There, at the age of eighteen, she took up with Mickey McCormick, a livery stable operator and professional gambler. Most nights she served as lookout girl for his faro bank in one or another of the saloons. Eventually they were married, at the suggestion of Justice of the Peace Wilson, and lived happily together until Mickey's death in 1912. Because, as she said, she wanted to be near his grave—and perhaps because she had nowhere else to go—Frenchy stayed on for nearly thirty more years in the adobe shanty Mickey had built for them. Reporters from the Amarillo papers interviewed her from time to time, but none ever learned her maiden name, or how she managed to pay for clothes and groceries. There may have been some savings from the gambling tables, but it is more likely that neighboring ranchers and their hands made occasional discreet contributions. As the last living relic of Tascosa, she may have aroused memories that were more romantic in retrospect than the town ever was in fact. The shanty did not survive for long after her death in 1941.

It is possible to add a more cheerful postscript. In 1939 Julian Bivins, son of Lee Bivins and then owner of much of the ranch land along the Canadian, gave the courthouse and 120 acres surrounding it to a group of Amarillo businessmen who were interested in founding a home and training school for orphaned, deserted, and delinquent boys. The group was led by Cal Farley, a one-time championship welterweight wrestler, who devoted much of his time and fortune to the rescue of such children.

Cal Farley's Boys' Ranch now covers the whole site of old Tascosa, and its population of about four hundred boys at any one time probably outnumbers the permanent residents of the original town. The boys helped build many of the fifty-odd dormitories, school buildings, vocational workshops, barns, and other facilities; they do most of the maintenance and house-keeping work; and on the forty-one hundred acres that the ranch now owns they raise much of their food, including beef, lamb, and pork. Since the ranch opened it has given a new start in life to more than three thousand youngsters from all parts of the country. All had been labeled by someone as "antisocial," "disturbed," or "delinquent," and more than half had been in trouble with the police. The present staff believes that at least 95 percent of the ranch's graduates have become solid citizens. I am glad that a dormitory is named Fischer Home, after one of my uncles.

The old courthouse is now the Julian Bivins Museum, housing a small collection of Indian and cowboy artifacts—plus, some of the boys claim, an occasional ghost.

SEVEN

Barbed Wire and the Art of Stringing It

If you grew up in a city, it is possible that you have never had occasion to look closely at a barbed-wire fence. In that case, it might be fun to try to invent it, in imagination, for yourself. It sounds easy. You only have to set two posts in the ground and string wires between them, fitted with barbs at about six-inch intervals. The problem is to fix the barbs so firmly that a heavy animal brushing against the fence will not break them off, or slide them along the wire. If they slide, you will soon have all the barbs shoved up against one post or the other, with a naked wire in between. Another problem is to figure out a way to make your wire cheaply and fast—that is, with machinery requiring a minimum of hand labor.

You might think of soldering on the barbs, but that quickly turns out to be a poor idea. The soldered join is inherently weak, and since each one has to be made by hand, the process would be prohibitively expensive. Another possibility is to take a ribbon of steel about one inch wide, cut zigzags along one side to form sharp points, and then twist the ribbon as you string it. This, too, has been tried and found impractical. The ribbon can be rolled, and cut by machinery, but it is too heavy to handle easily, uses too much expensive steel per foot, and is too weak to resist the impact of a charging bull. Another abortive scheme involved spiked spools strung on a wire.

According to the Bivins Museum in Tascosa, 401 patents for barbed wire have been recorded, and more than 1,600 variants have been catalogued. Out of all these attempts, only two proved successful. Both were patented at nearly the same time by two neighbors in De Kalb County, Illinois—Joseph F. Glidden and Jacob Haish. Whether they got their ideas independently, and who got his first, are questions that have provoked much expensive litigation. Their concepts were quite similar. Each involved clasping barbs around a wire at appropriate intervals—and then twisting that wire together with another one, so that the barbs are tightly gripped between the two. The only essential difference, to the eye of anyone but a patent lawyer, was in slightly variant methods of clasping the barb.

Whether or not Glidden was the original inventor, he certainly was the more successful businessman. He made his first wire in 1873, forming the barbs with a converted coffee grinder and twisting the twin wires in his barn with a hand-cranked grindstone. He sold his first wire, and took out his patent, in 1874. That same year he formed a partnership with a neighbor, I. L. Ellwood, and built a factory in De Kalb. Before the end of the next year, their factory was turning out five tons of wire a day, using improved, steam-operated machinery. In 1876 Glidden sold a half interest in his invention to the Washburn and Moen Manufacturing Company of Worcester, Massachusetts, which had been supplying him with plain wire; in payment he got $60,000, plus a royalty of twenty-five cents for every hundredweight of barbed wire sold.*

* Washburn and Moen eventually merged with the American Steel and Wire Company, a subsidiary of U.S. Steel. Its museum in Worcester is the prime source of information about barbed wire.

How profitable this deal proved to be can be glimpsed from the following figures. In his first year of manufacture, Glidden sold 10,000 pounds of wire. Two years later, Washburn and Moen sold 2.84 million pounds. Within the next five years, sales mounted to more than 80 million pounds a year—yielding Glidden an income of more than $200,000 annually, the equivalent of at least a million today, and that was before the era of income taxes. The manufacturers' profits amounted to many times that.

Much of his wire was being shipped to Texas. Glidden and his money followed it, leaving a permanent impress on the settlement of the High Plains and especially on its main city, Amarillo. There I came across his traces nearly sixty years later.

But in the meantime I had a chance to become well acquainted with his product. When I was eleven years old, my grandfather, John Fischer, taught me how to string wire during a summer I spent on his homestead near Apache, Oklahoma. To my eyes he seemed a very old man, but he was still wiry, lean, hard muscled, and accustomed to working from sunup till long after dark.

Like inventing barbed wire, stringing it is a more complex business than you might think. First you find your posts. My grandfather insisted that they be either cedar, locust, or bois d'arc, also known as Osage orange. These woods will last in the ground for many years, while cottonwood or pine will rot quickly unless creosoted—and we had no creosote in those days. Some he cut himself along a little creek that ran across one corner of his 160-acre farm; others he bought or bartered from neighbors. Each post had to be exactly six feet long.

When the posts were all collected, with a mule team and wagon, he stacked them near the edge of the pasture he planned to fence, and then marked his line. This he did with a borrowed surveyor's transit, a handful of stakes, and a few rolls of binder twine. At thirty-foot intervals he scratched a mark on the hard prairie soil to indicate where he wanted each post to go. One of my jobs was to make a hole in the ground with a crowbar at each mark, and fill it with water from a five-gallon, galvanized-iron milk can, thus softening the earth for my grandfather who followed me with his post-hole digger.

The first post set, to a depth of precisely two feet, was of course at a corner of the tract he was going to enclose. It had to be braced in both directions of the future fence lines. For braces he used two other posts planted diagonally in the earth with their feet anchored against heavy stones; their top ends he sawed at the proper angle and fastened to the corner post with tenpenny nails. Then we set about the weary labor of digging holes and setting intermediate posts until we came to the place he had marked for his next corner. We had to do only three sides of the forty-acre pasture, because the fourth side abutted a field enclosed years earlier; but, at that, the post setting took us the best part of two weeks.

Then we drove the wagon into Apache to get a load of wire. It came on big wooden spools, so heavy that the hardware dealer had to help us load them. Grandfather let me drive back, a proud and nervous assignment for me, although the mules—named Pete and Repeat—were gentle enough.

At the rear end of the wagon bed he rigged a pole, crosswise, to serve as a spindle on which a spool of wire could be mounted and easily unwound. We drove the wagon close to a corner post, twisted the end of the wire around it one foot above the ground and stapled it fast. Next we drove along the line of posts for about two hundred yards, unreeling wire on the ground behind us. There Grandfather stopped, unhitched the team, blocked three wheels of the wagon with rocks, and jacked up the fourth wheel, the rear one next to the fence line. He cut the wire and twisted the loose end around the axle of the jacked-up wheel, fastening it to a spoke for additional security. By turning the wheel, we wound the wire around the axle until it was taut. (There were patent wire stretchers, but Grandpa did not own one. The wheel-stretching method worked just as well, and saved money.) After he had lashed the wheel to maintain the tension, we went back down the line and stapled the wire to each post. Then we repeated the process, time after time, until we had the pasture enclosed with a standard fence of four strands, spaced a foot apart. We finished up by making a wire gate at the corner nearest the house.

Three tips for fence stringers:

1. Wear the heaviest leather gauntlets you can find. Even so, you are bound to get your hands and arms torn, so carry some iodine and bandages with you.
2. Staple the wire on the side of the posts facing into the pasture. When a heavy animal runs into the fence, he will press the wire against the posts, not the staples. If the wire were on the other side, the staples might pop out.
3. Hang the expense, and use two staples for each fastening of the wire. One of them might someday rust or work loose.

I haven't seen that fence in decades, but my brother told me a few years ago that it was still standing and tight. It is, probably, the most nearly permanent thing I have ever worked on. Certainly its useful life has been far longer than that of any article or book I have written.

While we strung wire, I peppered Grandpa with endless questions. The answers I got were sometimes unexpected. For example, I had never imagined that for some people war could be fun. This fact also seems to have escaped the stuffier generals, such as Sherman. (Not Lee. He believed it was fortunate that war was so bloody, lest men learn to like it too much. And until the Battle of Yellow Tavern, Jeb Stuart evidently regarded the whole thing as a wonderful lark.)

As my grandfather Fischer told it, the Civil War was a four-year picnic, with fireworks. No doubt the old man's memory had, in the usual fashion, filtered out the most unpleasant experiences; but I think it likely that those years really were the most interesting he ever had. One of his comments I remember verbatim.

"The saddest day of my life up till that time," he said, "was the day the navy paid me off and sent me back to the farm."

He had been born in 1850 beside the Ohio River, on a farm near Marietta, and from the time he was old enough to lift a hoe, he had looked with envy at the deck hands lounging on the rail of the paddle-wheelers that steamed past. So, when the war came, he enlisted at the age of ten as a cabin boy on one of Commodore Foote's gunboats. There he ate better than he ever had in his life; one of America's oldest military traditions is that the navy gets better food, and more of it, than the army. His duties were not arduous. And the river sailors, sheltered behind their armor of boiler plate and railway rails, took relatively few casualties.

Cabin boy John Fischer got his only wound, his wildest party, and his worst disgrace in the Vicksburg campaign. He had left his gunboat to volunteer for service on one of the transports that Adm. David Porter had chosen for the supposedly desperate race down the Mississippi under the muzzles of the Vicksburg batteries on the night of April 16, 1863. When he first told me about it, I had no way of making notes, but I jotted some down later and believe that what follows is an essentially accurate, though necessarily reconstructed, account.

"Everybody except Grant and Porter thought the scheme was crazy," he said. "While I was cleaning up the officers' mess, I heard them say that even Sherman was against it, and that all our unarmored transports were bound to be sunk before we could steam a hundred yards beyond the Big Bend. All that afternoon I helped stack cotton bales and barrels of hardtack along the rails, to give the deck hands a little cover. They made a mighty flimsy breastwork, and I figured I would never live to see morning.

"What really happened was a sort of anticlimax. The night

was real dark, and of course there wasn't a single candle or
seegar alight in our whole string of ships. Besides, we stuck
close to the west bank so the Reb gunners couldn't see us too
well, even after they had set fire to some barns and houses to
light up the river.

"But they sure tried. For nearly two hours they blazed away
with all the cannon they could bring to bear, and I guess maybe
ten thousand riflemen kept popping at us as fast as they could
load. I watched the whole thing through a crack between two
cotton bales, jumping like a rabbit every time a cannonball
slammed into our boat. One transport ran aground and sank,
and most of the others got splintered up pretty bad—but we
didn't lose a man.

"Seemed like I was always hungry those days, like a teen-age
boy generally is, so as soon as the shooting was over, I slipped
along the deck till I found a smashed cracker barrel. I started
eating hardtack as fast as I could stuff it into my mouth, aiming
to get my fill before an officer caught me. In the dark I
couldn't see that a Minié ball had stuck in one of those crack-
ers, and I broke a tooth. It wasn't what you could call a glorious
wound, I guess, but it *was* caused by an enemy weapon."

Toward the end of the campaign some of the transports
were ordered to Natchez for repair. In those days Natchez was
two towns—a dignified cluster of porticoed mansions on the
bluff, and below it a rowdy port, Natchez-Under-the-Hill.

"The moment we tied up," Grandpa said, "every man aboard
lit out for the saloons, which were loud and plentiful. But the
captain told me and Henry that the cabin boys would have to
stay and look after the ship. He also ordered us to have plenty
of hot coffee ready by daybreak, on the theory that he and the
other officers would need it when they got back.

"Neither of us knew much about cooking, but we filled a ten-
gallon wash boiler full of water and ten pounds of coffee and
set it on the galley stove. By midnight it was boiling good, but
an awful lot of coffee grounds seemed to be floating on the top.

"Now somewhere I had heard that eggshells would settle coffee grounds. Henry argued that didn't stand to reason. What the situation called for was something with more body to it, like whole eggs. So we broke a dozen eggs in the boiler and stirred for a while. That helped some, but not much. So we added another dozen, and threw in the shells after them.

"Naturally we were pretty sore about missing the fun in Natchez-Under-the-Hill, and when Henry found a bottle of vanilla extract in the pantry, we decided to have a party of our own. Come daylight, we were smelling like a pair of angel food cakes. At about that point it occurred to us that the coffee better be real good when the captain got home. We broke in all the rest of the eggs in the galley, including those that weren't too fresh, and were stirring hard when the officers wobbled up the gangplank.

"In spite of all the pains we had taken, the captain wasn't happy about that coffee. In fact, he was downright irritable. Said we had tried to poison him. Said we were probably Rebel spies. Said that we were anyhow no-good brats, and we would sure God spend the rest of the war in the brig.

"Maybe we would have, too, if the officers hadn't got tired of waiting on their own table. We never were officially pardoned, exactly, but the first officer let us out in time to see the surrender at Vicksburg in July."

For officers in general, my grandfather had scant respect. Sherman, for example, he described as "a nervous old fussbudget" who nearly lost the whole Army of Tennessee at Shiloh out of sheer carelessness, and who was saved only by the last-minute arrival of the river flotilla with fire power and reinforcements. But Grant, he admitted, "probably knew what he was up to." Sometimes he added that "Grant wasn't as flighty as most of them generals"—a rare compliment from the old man, who regarded flightiness (or any other display of emotion) with chill contempt.

This judgment apparently was based less on Grant's record of victories than on a cabin boy's observation of his behavior under fire. Grandpa's best chance for a close-up appraisal came at the siege of Fort Donelson. For hours there the gunboats tossed shells into the Confederate entrenchments while Grant watched from the river bank a few yards away. The weather was near freezing, and an icy rain fell at intervals through the day.

"He scootched up in his saddle like a wet chicken," Grandpa remembered, "while the water dripped down his coat collar, and now and then a Reb cannonball splashed mud over his boots."

For his juvenile listener, this was exciting stuff. I nagged for details. What I wanted, I suppose, though I didn't know how to ask for it, was an insight into the character of a hero, some explanation of what it is that makes a great man great. What did Grant do to win the battle?

"He didn't do anything so far as I could see," Grandpa said. "He just sat there like a hickory stump."

Well, then, how did he *really* look?

"He looked cold."

At the time these answers seemed unsatisfactory to me, but years later I began to suspect that they summed up the basic facts about Grant pretty well—a cold man, unbudgeable as a hickory stump.

Again, I found out years later that my two grandfathers must have been on opposite sides in at least two battles—Shiloh and Donelson—and probably at Fort Henry. But it is most unlikely that they ever got within shooting distance, and they never did meet, on the battlefield or elsewhere.

Incidentally, the Civil War was the last major conflict fought without benefit of Glidden's formidable weapon, barbed wire. As much of it must have been strung in France during World War I as ever was used in Texas.

Nobody could have been more foreign to the ethos of Tascosa, or the Caperton family, than Grandfather Fischer. He was a farmer, not a cattleman; I never saw him on horseback. The Capertons had some pretensions to aristocratic descent. (They had inherited from an uncertain source a coat of arms bearing a chevron, three boars' heads, and a Gaelic inscription no one could read. My mother always insisted it must have been: "Root, hog, or die.") The Fischers were descended from a German peasant who fled from Hesse-Darmstadt in 1848, after a wave of abortive revolutions had swept Europe. Family tradition held that he fought with the rebels, and faced prison or execution if he had not escaped to the New World. Grandpa Fischer had no use for firearms, or those who carried them. Except for that juvenile experiment with vanilla extract, I think he never took a drink in his life. He was a religious man, who read a chapter of the Bible every evening and raised his thirteen children with stern authority. His wife had died before I was born. He then decreed that his youngest daughter, Jennie, should not marry because it was her duty to stay on the homestead and look after him. He experimented endlessly with different crops, to discover what would grow best in that harsh climate. One of them was broom corn, which he sold to the state prison at McAlester, where some of the inmates made brooms. He was skilled in several crafts, from carpentry to blacksmithing. Watching him make a wagon bed, I once asked him why he bothered to plane it so carefully on the bottom, which would be out of sight. Who would know if it wasn't perfectly finished?

"I would know," he said, "and God would know."

In sum, he was a prototype of the small-scale family farmers who eventually took over much of the prairie from the cattlemen who originally settled it. Even the High Plains are now planted to wheat, cotton, and maize wherever there is enough rainfall or pumpable ground water to make a crop. This kind of settlement would, of course, have been impossible without Glidden's fencing.

In the late twenties my father ran, as a sideline, an abstract and title company in Amarillo. It nicely supplemented his main business, which was trading land and investing money for Eastern life insurance companies in farm mortgages. Often I helped out, after school and on weekends, mostly by tracing out land titles in the deed record books at the courthouse. Dull work, usually, although some of the older surveys did have points of interest. They were often expressed in exotic terms— "Spanish leagues"—or such directions as "Ride five hours west from Torrey Peaks, then turn north to the Canadian River." Another common measurement was the *vara,* or thirty-three inches—the length of a Spanish cavalry saber, and by coincidence also about the length of the stride of the average trotting pony. Thus a cowboy riding at a trot could measure off the boundary of a pasture by counting his horse's steps. Such measurements were, obviously, far from precise, and later led to many lawsuits, clouded titles, and resurveys.

The name I encountered most often in the property records was Glidden and Sanborn. When Glidden began to manufacture barbed wire, he soon realized he needed a salesman. The best he could find was Henry B. Sanborn, a New Yorker who had become a successful horse trader, working out of Denver. Glidden appointed him and his partner, Dudley P. Warner, as general agents for the sale of wire throughout the West. They began their venture by building a temporary wire pen in the main plaza of San Antonio and stocking it with Mexican yearling cattle. It was within plain sight of the Southern Hotel and the Hole-in-the-Wall saloon, then the main gathering places for cattlemen of that part of Texas. When they saw that the pen held the half-wild animals securely, and without injury beyond an odd scratch, they were convinced. That pen—and others like it in Houston, Dallas, and Sherman—sold more wire than any conceivable advertisement.

As he became rich, Glidden formed a separate partnership with Sanborn, primarily for investment in Western real estate. Together they started the Frying Pan ranch, partly as a demonstration, partly as a successful venture into the cattle business. When the railroads began to build into the Texas Panhandle, they decided to expand into city real estate—for it was clear to everyone that a thriving town would soon develop wherever the first two rail lines might cross.

A land speculator and town-site developer from Abilene, J. T. Berry, thought he knew a likely place. In 1887 he bought a section of state land alongside the proposed route of the Fort Worth & Denver Railway, then building diagonally across the Panhandle from southeast to northwest. For the 640 acres he paid $1,280, or about twice what it had been worth as range land. His tract bordered on Wild Horse Lake, what the geologists call a "playa," or dish-shaped depression caused by subsistence of the underlying bedrock. Such shallow ponds are fairly common on the High Plains. They range from a few yards to a mile wide, and after a heavy rain they may hold a few feet of water for several months. In prolonged dry spells they disappear, leaving only a patch of dry, sun-crackled mud. Nevertheless, when they hold any water at all, they are a valuable asset to cattlemen in a country where running streams may be eighty miles apart. Berry's lake was conveniently located between the Canadian River and the Palo Duro Canyon. He figured it would be a good place to water the cattle, which he hoped would be driven to his new town for shipment by rail. Berry called his town site Amarillo, the Spanish term for "yellow," because it was near an arroyo, or dry gulch, with yellow banks.

Glidden and Sanborn decided that they wanted a piece of action in this new settlement—or, better yet, to take it over for themselves. They encouraged their foreman on the Frying Pan ranch, W. W. Wetzel, to build a home there—he was later to become its first mayor—and they bought four sections of land just to the east of Berry's site. This they named the Glidden and Sanborn addition to Amarillo.

Berry gave lots within his town site to about sixty cowboys working on the LX ranch, with the understanding that they, as freeholders, would vote to make Amarillo the county seat of Potter County, a new unit of government that he was then organizing. An election to confirm these arrangements was held on August 6, 1887, at the LX headquarters. The following month the newly elected county commissioners voted to appropriate twenty-five dollars from the first tax money collected to buy a tent, table, and chairs to serve as a temporary office for their county clerk. Within a year, thanks to Berry's energy, Amarillo had a brick courthouse, a saloon, several stores, a post office, two windmills, a railway depot, a stockyard with loading chutes, and a handful of clapboard houses.

From Glidden and Sanborn's point of view, there was only one thing wrong with this budding settlement—it was on Berry's property, not theirs. They promptly launched a campaign to move the town, with Sanborn acting as field general and Glidden putting up the money. Sanborn's opening gambit was to build a home for himself, the most pretentious in the county, on what is now the site of the Amarillo City Center. He also built a hotel, the finest in the Panhandle, donated lots for a church site, and began to trade lots in the Glidden and Sanborn addition for property on the Berry site—paying the cost of moving the house for any family willing to shift its residence. Sanborn got an unexpected reinforcement from the weather. The winter of 1888 turned out to be unusually wet, so that Wild Horse Lake overflowed into the Berry site—while the Glidden and Sanborn addition, on higher ground, remained dry.

Sanborn's decisive maneuver to shift the location of Amarillo took place in Chicago, at the general offices of the Sante Fe Railway. That line was also building into the Panhandle, with tentative plans to intersect with the Fort Worth & Denver at Washburn, a tiny village about sixteen miles east of Amarillo. Sanborn sent his lawyer, S. H. Madden, to Chicago to persuade the railroad managers to aim for Amarillo instead. As an inducement, he promised to raise enough money to build a terminal there—and he pointed out that shipments of Glidden's wire could provide a great deal of freight traffic for any railroad that proved cooperative. That argument apparently tipped the balance, thus determining the future economic geography of north Texas. After the Santa Fe built into Amarillo, it was inevitable that a third railroad, the Rock Island, would lay its tracks through that junction as well. All three lines eventually established their depots in the Glidden and Sanborn addition, and in 1893 the courthouse was moved there, too, leaving the original Berry town site virtually abandoned. Sanborn not only had kidnapped, in effect, the town of Amarillo, he had also doomed its potential rival.

Washburn is now literally only a wide place in the road—on highway 287 and not far from Interstate 40. Its only distinction is an architectural curiosity, the only wooden grain elevator remaining (so far as I can learn) on the High Plains. Meanwhile, Amarillo has become the capital of an economic empire sprawling over parts of five states. Visually it offers an experience unlike any other city. As you drive toward it from the east, through an apparently endless, flat sea of grass and wheat, its towers begin to loom up on the horizon like the sails of a distant fleet. The clear atmosphere gives you the illusion that you are almost there—but you will drive on for another half-hour as the towers grow larger and gradually take on definition as grain elevators and office buildings. Once you reach its suburbs, the dreck of filling stations, motels, eateries, and used-car lots is as unsightly as the outskirts of any other American city—

but from, say, twenty miles, Amarillo is spectacularly lovely. I have often wished that Mr. Glidden and Mr. Sanborn could have had such a glimpse of the community they did so much to found.

EIGHT

Geronimo's Magic Blanket

When I got my first training as an artilleryman at Fort Sill, Oklahoma, everybody around there knew that Geronimo had once owned a magic blanket. The old warrior had taken up enforced residence at Fort Sill in his declining years, and though he had been dead for nearly two decades when I arrived, many people on the post and in the nearby towns of Lawton and Apache remembered him well.

During his long years on the warpath, Geronimo had assembled his blanket, like a piece quilt, out of white women's scalps—ninety-nine of them, according to the most frequent account. It was warm and fashionable—the envy of every chief between the Gila River and the Arapaho country—but it was a nuisance to keep well groomed on the march because of its tendency to collect sandburs and fleas. Moreover, as the Southwest became infested with Gen. George Crook's cavalry, the owner realized that it was becoming increasingly hard to replace (or even patch up) if he wore it out.

So eventually he reserved it strictly for urgent magical uses, with splendid results. When spread over a wounded brave, it would heal him faster than rattlesnake oil or any other available medication. At night, it would make the wearer invisible, so that he could steal horses from the best-guarded remuda. Worn in battle, it would deflect the slugs from a Winchester carbine, as Geronimo himself demonstrated on many occasions. He would never have surrendered, if his women and children had not been starving. He could never resist a squaw's tears.

All this Geronimo had related to visitors as he sat on a bench in the winter sunshine outside his stone cell in the old barracks. Often on such occasions he cuddled on his knee the five-year-old daughter of an artillery instructor. She was fond of him, and he loved to stroke her blond curls.

This story was first told to me by my grandfather Fischer during one of our stretches of fence building. I am sure he believed it, because he was not a fanciful man and so far as I know he never told me an untruth. (Well, once maybe, but only in fun. When I asked him how fireflies made their light, he looked thoughtful for a few minutes and then said: "They gnash their teeth to make sparks.") The tale remained current for many years, and cropped up from time to time in Oklahoma newspapers. Probably it originated with Geronimo himself; he was a notorious liar, and in his later years the enhancement of his reputation for ferocity had a cash value. Though nominally a prisoner, he was then permitted to travel to fairs and Wild West shows, where he emitted blood-chilling war whoops and sold autographed snapshots for $1.50. For these exhibitions he usually wore a Sioux costume, since it was showier than the clothes of the Apaches, who did not go in for such fripperies as war bonnets, feathers, and wampum belts. When practicing their trade, they did not wear anything except war paint, moccasins, a breechclout, and a cloth headband to keep sweat out of their eyes.

The only trouble with the magic-blanket story is that it is almost certainly not true. To begin with, the Apaches usually did not take scalps, as the Comanches and other Plains tribes did. Moreover, no mention of such a blanket is made in any of the original accounts of Geronimo's pursuit. It was not with him at the time of his final surrender, no reliable witness ever claimed to have seen it, and Jason Betzinez, who fought with Geronimo and shared his captivity, flatly denies that tale in his memoir, the best account of the Apache wars by an Indian participant.* Reluctantly, I had to conclude that it is only one of the many legends that grew up around Geronimo. Others were (1) that he was the greatest of the Apache chiefs; (2) that he was a hero in the eyes of his own people; (3) that his name was Geronimo.

Actually, he had no hereditary claim to the title of chief, and he never led more than a small band of raiders. His stature did not compare with that of the tribe's great leaders, such as Mangas Coloradas, Cochise, Victorio, and Juh. Many Apaches disliked and mistrusted him, most refused to join in his depredations, and in 1885 two of his comrades tried to kill him when they discovered he had lied to them. In the end, it was Apache scouts employed by the United States Army who were responsible for his capture. Furthermore, Geronimo had nine wives and mistreated them all. Whenever he could get his hands on liquor—either *tiswin*, an Indian beer made from corn mash, or bootleg whiskey—he drank himself into a stupor. In February 1909 he got so drunk he fell off his horse, lay all night in a patch of damp weeds, and died of pneumonia a few days later in the Fort Sill hospital.

His real name was Goyakla, which means "One Who Yawns"—reputedly because he yawned a lot when he was a baby. Geronimo was a nickname given him by the Mexican soldiers who fought against him; they pronounced it "Hieronomo."

*Jason Betzinez with Wilbur S. Nye, *I Fought with Geronimo,* (Harrisburg, Pa.: Stackpole Co., 1959). This is now a rare item of Western Americana.

But one facet of his legendary reputation is deserved. He was indisputably one of the most talented guerrilla fighters who ever lived. One of his enemies, Lt. Britton Davis of the U.S. Third Cavalry, in writing of the final pursuit of Geronimo's band, paid him this tribute:

> In this campaign thirty-five men and eight half-grown or older boys, encumbered with the care and sustenance of 101 women and children, with no base of supplies and no means of waging war or of obtaining food or transportation other than what they could take from their enemies, maintained themselves for eighteen months in a country two hundred by four hundred miles in extent, against five thousand troops, regulars and irregulars, five hundred Indian auxiliaries of these troops, and an unknown number of civilians.*

He might have added that Geronimo at the time was already an old man by Indian standards—more than fifty, although no one (including himself) was ever sure of his birth date. He was fighting over some of the cruelest terrain of this continent, almost barren of both food and water. He had marched something over two thousand miles, much of it on foot, sometimes covering fifty miles a day. He was never captured; he made a negotiated surrender to Gen. Nelson Miles, then commanding the American forces. And when the cease-fire was agreed upon, Geronimo still had with him twenty-one men and thirteen women.

He had also kept his sense of humor. The translator who was helping to negotiate the surrender said, in an effort at diplomacy: "General Miles is your friend."

"I have been in need of friends lately," Geronimo replied. "Where has he been?"

With those words, on September 6, 1886, at Camp Bowie, Arizona, Geronimo ended the last Indian outbreak in the United States and his own career of thirty-five years of almost continuous warfare. He had been trained for his profession

* Lt. Britton Davis, *The Truth About Geronimo* (New Haven: Yale University Press, 1929).

from his earliest boyhood in the Sierra Madre mountains of northern Mexico, the stronghold of the Chiricahua Apaches. They were one of the many bands, or subtribes, of Apaches that roamed through Sonora, Chihuahua, New Mexico, and Arizona, making only occasional contact with each other. At one time the Apaches had dominated the High Plains of Texas as well, but were driven toward the South and West during the early years of the eighteenth century by an invasion of the more numerous Comanches. During Geronimo's boyhood, they still returned to the High Plains from time to time to hunt buffalo, steal Comanche horses, and raid white settlements and wagon trains. Even among the other Apaches, the Chiricahuas had a reputation for peculiar ferocity. For at least two hundred years, and probably much longer, they had been predators, a way of life that had become as natural to them as it is to the hawk or rattlesnake. Their earliest victims were the farming and livestock-raising Indians, such as the Hopi and Pueblos. Later they specialized in Mexicans. One historian, E. M. Halliday, has noted that they "hunted Mexicans almost as the Plains Indians hunted buffalo; they seemed to be natural prey . . ."*

The Chiricahuas were more primitive than most tribes of the Southwest. They raised nothing, wove no blankets, and had no permanent homes, not even a buffalo-hide tepee. They lived in wickiups, crude brush shelters that they abandoned every time they changed campsites. Their diet ranged from field mice to horse meat, together with a few berries, cactus fruits, and the heart of the mescal, or century plant—plus, of course, anything they could loot from Mexican farms and villages. Although they were competent horsemen, they did not collect large herds, as the Comanches did, and showed no particular affection for their mounts. Often they would ride a horse to exhaustion and then butcher it; it was always easy to steal another.

*E. M. Halliday, *Geronimo!* (New York: American Heritage Publishing Co., 1966).

Raiding was both their business and their chief pleasure. Boys were trained for it from about the age of five, learning to handle weapons, to conceal themselves in the scantiest cover, and to endure long marches through the roughest mountains, where mounted pursuers could not follow. From these fastnesses they would swoop down on a wagon train or Mexican settlement, seize any goods they fancied—particularly rifles and ammunition—and disappear again into the Sierra Madre. Occasionally they took with them children and younger women for adoption into the tribe. All adult males they encountered were either killed on the spot or taken back to camp for a few days of torture. This rite, or sport, was usually performed by women who had lost sons or husbands in some earlier raid. On the rare occasions when Mexican cavalry were able to ambush an Apache band, they seldom took prisoners either.

According to the tribe's custom, Geronimo was taken on his first raid at the age of fifteen, as an apprentice warrior. He and the other neophytes were kept out of danger as much as possible, but were expected to do sentry duty, look after the horses and plunder, and observe carefully the tactics of their elders. After four such raids—if he survived, and had behaved with courage and discipline—a boy was considered a graduate, entitled to fight alongside the grownups and share equally in their takings. According to his own account, and Betzinez's, Geronimo passed the test with distinction. He soon married and fathered three children; they and his wife were all killed by Mexican soldiers in an encounter near Janos, Chihuahua, in 1858.

To console Geronimo, Mangas Coloradas appointed him to plan and lead a retaliatory attack the following year. He was notably successful, routing four companies of Mexican troops with heavy casualties; it was in this battle that the Mexicans gave him the nickname that he used for the rest of his life. From then on he led marauding parties, usually of thirty to fifty men, on the raids that made him notorious on both sides of the border.

For the Chiricahuas made the mistake of extending their forays into Arizona and New Mexico. Their main purpose was to get Winchester repeating rifles, which were far superior to the old-fashioned single-shot Mexican army muskets. Once so equipped, they had to make frequent follow-up expeditions to get Winchester cartridges, unobtainable in Mexico. On the way they naturally stole cattle, burned ranches, pillaged mining camps, and murdered any settlers they happened to meet. This carefree behavior had two unfortunate consequences. The less militant bands of Apaches living in Arizona and New Mexico often got blamed for the misdeeds of the Chiricahuas, since most Americans could not tell one Apache from another, nor guess where a raiding party came from. Moreover, the local settlers began to pelt Washington with a hailstorm of protests and demands for protection—preferably by the extermination of all Apaches, or at the very least by confining them to reservations.

In response, Washington sent out Gen. George Crook, the most brilliant army officer who ever dealt with the Indians. Unlike most Americans of that time, he actually liked Indians, treated them fairly, tried to protect them against unscrupulous white traders and land grabbers, and always tried conciliation before he used force. In return, most Indians—including the more tractable of the Apaches—came to respect and eventually to love him, as Betzinez has testified.

In July 1871 Crook began a highly unconventional campaign. His purpose was to get all the Apaches to live on reservations in Arizona and New Mexico, and to persuade them to take to farming rather than marauding. His method was a judicious combination of negotiation, together with a show of force—and, as a last resort, the relentless use of force. He promised the Indians land, government rations until they learned to raise their own food, and—for the chiefs and better warriors—employment as army scouts. Most of the Apaches living north of the Mexican border accepted this offer, but those south of it did not. Crook was determined either to bring them in or wipe them out.

The idea of arming Apaches to hunt other Apaches struck most Arizonans as crazy and dangerous, but it worked, for two main reasons. Many Indian bands disapproved of Geronimo because he was causing trouble for the whole tribe. They also realized, earlier than he did, that the predator business was about played out; service as army scouts promised to be almost as much fun, and had a more auspicious future. So it was that men who had once fought alongside Geronimo became indispensable allies of Crook. One of them, Tso-ay—whom the Americans called Peaches, because of his light complexion—turned out to be a winning card; he knew the secret way into Geronimo's Sierra Madre base camp.

Crook held another ace. For the first time the Mexican and American governments had agreed that U.S. troops could cross into Mexico if they were in hot pursuit of hostile Indians. So Crook started south on May 1, 1883, with 235 men, all but 42 of them friendly Apaches. They traveled light—each man carried only his rifle, one blanket, a canteen, and forty rounds of ammunition, while a mule train followed with rations and camp equipment.

Meanwhile, Geronimo was having trouble enough with Mexican troops, who were pressing him harder than they ever had before. Once they ambushed his band, with its families, while it was moving along the foothills of the Sierra. Many Indians were killed in the first attack, but Geronimo, with thirty-two surviving warriors and a few women and children, managed to make a stand in a dry gulch. There they dug rifle pits and held off the soldiers through a day of hard fighting. Here is how Betzinez told the rest of the story:

After dark [the Mexicans] set fire to the grass, hoping to burn the Indians out. The latter were now in a serious condition. They were surrounded by the prairie fire, the circle of it drawing closer. The warriors asked the consent of the few women who were there to let them choke the small children so that they wouldn't give away their movements by crying. Then they all crawled through the fire and got away without being seen . . . We lost nearly half our families in this tragedy.

The Mexican commander, Col. Lorenzo Garcia, later claimed that the Apaches lost seventy-eight killed and about thirty prisoners, while his own casualties came to less than half of that. Later expeditions by Geronimo's people into Sonora and Chihuahua were less costly, but the band was dwindling steadily, and rarely had a chance to rest. With discouragement and bad temper beginning to simmer, the warriors began to quarrel among themselves. And Geronimo began to have premonitions.

"We were sitting there eating," Betzinez related.

Geronimo was sitting next to me with a knife in one hand and a chunk of beef which I had cooked for him in the other. All at once he dropped the knife, saying, "Men, our people whom we left at our base camp are now in the hands of U.S. troops! What shall we do?"

This was a startling example of Geronimo's mysterious ability to tell what was happening at a distance. I cannot explain it to this day. But I was there and I saw it. No, he did not get the word by some messenger. And no smoke signals had been made.

Geronimo's prophecy was correct. In less than two weeks, Crook's party, guided by Peaches, had penetrated into the heart of the Sierra Madre, climbing through mountains no white man had ever seen. The trails were so narrow and rough that five mules fell over cliffs to their death, but Crook did not lose a man. At a height of about eight thousand feet, the troops came upon a small hidden valley, which Peaches identified as Geronimo's favorite campsite. It was empty—but a few days later a detachment of scouts surprised another encampment not far away. There they killed a few old Apache men, dispersed a few others, and captured four children and a young woman. She told Crook that the Indians were "astounded and dismayed" when they realized that the Americans had found their way into the stronghold—and she predicted that several raiding parties then out, including Geronimo's, would be willing to discuss a truce when they returned.

Crook sent her out to meet the returning warriors with the bad news. Within a day or two, old men, women, and children began to make their way nervously into the American lines; and before the end of the month several bands of raiders came in to lay down their rifles. Among them was Geronimo, who had finally decided that enough was enough. At least for the time being.

Geronimo had no serious objection to a brief vacation on an American reservation. Twice before, in fact, he had lived for brief periods on the Mimbres and San Carlos reservations, leaving without difficulty when he felt like returning to Mexico and marauding. Doubtless he believed he could do so again. Besides, Crook's terms were attractive. The general promised fair treatment, no reprisals, and protection from the Arizona settlers who wanted to lynch any Apaches they could lay hands on. He even agreed to take the main body of Indians with him, but to let Geronimo, Juh, Chatto and a few other warriors remain behind for a few months to tidy up their unfinished business in the Sierra Madre. This business, they claimed, was to round up some Chiricahua stragglers who were supposed to be still at large. What they actually had in mind was a farewell raid on the Mexicans.

To the surprise of many Americans, Geronimo and his companions did show up at the San Carlos reservation, though a couple of months later than they had promised. They brought with them a large herd of stolen cattle. General Crook ordered the herd confiscated and sold at auction, and sent the proceeds back to Mexico for distribution among the farmers who had been plundered. Geronimo resented this bitterly for the rest of his life.

Nevertheless, he settled down on an allotment of land on Turkey Creek near Fort Apache and tried his hand at behaving like "the tame Indians," his contemptuous term for those who had joined the reservation earlier. He even learned something of that despised occupation, farming, although he let his current wives do most of the work. (There was a brisk turnover among Geronimo's wives.)

A recent television show portrayed Geronimo and his fellow Chiricahuas on the reservation as the victims of outrageous mistreatment, insult, and cheating at the hands of the whites. This is not the case. General Crook saw to it that they were treated fairly, and protected as much as possible from the ministrations of bootleggers and corrupt Indian agents. His charges were now under army jurisdiction, rather than that of the Department of the Interior, which supervised most reservations—and Betzinez reported that "all relations between ourselves and the troops were peaceful and harmonious."

Still, Geronimo had his grievances. The "tame" Indians were not very friendly to him. He felt insulted by articles about him published in the Arizona newspapers, which a translator had read to him. Lt. Britton Davis, in immediate charge of the Turkey Creek Indian settlement, had tried to stop Geronimo and a few of his drinking companions from brewing *tiswin*— contrary to a sensible regulation—and beating their wives. This the Apaches regarded as intolerable interference with their domestic affairs.

Above all, Geronimo was bored. So on May 17, 1885, after more than a year of the sedentary life, he slipped away from the reservation for the last time—thus touching off the last of the great Indian campaigns. He was able to persuade only thirty-four other warriors and something over a hundred women and children to go with him; many of his comrades from the old days in the Sierra Madre, including Chatto and Betzinez, refused to join a foray they considered harebrained and hopeless. Within hours, Lieutenant Davis, with a detachment of loyal Apache scouts and two troops of cavalry, was on the trail of the escapees, but he lost it the first night out.

Once more General Crook mobilized all his forces for a general pursuit, and alerted the Mexicans to do the same. But this campaign turned out to be quite different from previous ones. Geronimo avoided fighting whenever possible, knowing that he was hopelessly outnumbered. Instead he dodged back and forth across the border, hiding in the rugged country that he knew better than anybody, and evading both Mexican and American detachments. Whenever he camped, he designated a rallying point fifty or sixty miles away; then if his band was attacked, it dispersed like a flock of quail in all directions—under orders to regroup by ones and twos at the designated rendezvous a few days later. The pursuing soldiers had to follow a multiplicity of tracks, most of which they lost in the rocky terrain. At best they sometimes captured a few women and a couple of worn-out ponies. Another of Geronimo's tactics was to pitch false camps, each with a few wickiups, a smoldering fire, and a staked horse. He would then make his real camp a mile or two away, preferably on a mountain slope where he could watch the false camp from concealment. Often he enjoyed the spectacle of his pursuers stealthily surrounding the decoy and launching a futile attack. He was also a master at laying false trails and covering his real tracks.

Still, he could not escape all encounters. On one of his raids into Arizona to replenish ammunition, he was so closely followed by army detachments that, in the words of an official report, he "committed only fourteen murders" and lost several of his own men before vanishing again into the Mexican wilderness. The constant long, hard marches on short rations were wearing down even the toughest fighting men. And perhaps Geronimo was disheartened by the capture of his sixth wife and two small children by American troops in a skirmish in Sonora, and the loss of most of his horses and camp equipment in another. (Apparently the loss of the horses was the more serious, since he married a seventh wife while still on the run.) At any rate, in March 1886 he sent word to Crook that he wanted a conference.

The general, accompanied by only a few soldiers and a photographer,* met with Geronimo and his chief lieutenants for three days near San Bernardino Springs in northern Mexico. Most of the time was taken up with Geronimo's long-winded oratory, in which he tried to excuse his behavior and to blame everybody else; but in the end he agreed to give up. Crook returned to Arizona, leaving a detachment of troops and scouts to accompany the renegades back to the reservation. On the way, however, the party encountered a bootlegger; the prisoners got roaring drunk, forgot about their promises to Crook, and took off again for the mountains.

The campaign had already created an uproar in the American press. The tone of its editorials now rose a couple of octaves. The War Department was furious with Crook—understandably, though perhaps unjustly—for letting the old fox slip through his fingers. He was replaced in command by Gen. Nelson Miles, who took up the weary pursuit once more. One of his detachments under Capt. Henry W. Lawton eventually got so close that Geronimo again asked for a surrender conference—and this time the troops managed to get him all the way back to Miles's headquarters at Fort Bowie for a final submission.

From then on nobody was about to believe Geronimo's pledges, or to give him another chance to sneak back to Mexico. Along with the rest of the Chiricahuas, including those who had no part in his last outbreak, he was shipped off to Florida. When the weather there did not agree with the Indians, accustomed to a desert climate, they were moved to Alabama, and later to Fort Sill. There Geronimo again took up farming, in a desultory sort of way, and spent his last years in considerable

---

* C. S. Fly of Tombstone, Arizona, who got some excellent pictures of Geronimo and companions even before the surrender.

comfort. The military reservation then covered about seventy thousand acres, but had only a small garrison. There was plenty of room, therefore, for twelve Apache villages, located where streams, timber, and grazing land were most suitable. Each had a generous allotment for farming and cattle raising. After living for a few weeks in an old barracks on his arrival, Geronimo was appointed head of a village on Apache Creek, where his family and several close friends—including Betzinez—built wooden homes, the roomiest and most weather-tight they had ever known. Geronimo was also given the rank and uniform of a scout, in both of which he took great pride. Besides his pay as a scout, he earned a fair amount of money by his appearances in fairs and Wild West shows—enough so that he was able, in about 1905, to buy an early-model Buick. He delighted in driving his Apache friends around the reservation, often wearing a silk top hat to give him the proper touch of magnificence. Next to whiskey, vanity was always his greatest weakness.

While the Chiricahuas were still in the East, Betzinez had gone to the Indian School at Carlisle Barracks, Pennsylvania, where he learned English, Christianity, and blacksmithing, a trade that earned him a good living after the move to Fort Sill. Occasionally he shod mules for my grandfather, whose homestead was only a few miles from the Apache Creek settlement. He married a white woman, who had come to Fort Sill as a missionary, and both of them became prominent members of the First Presbyterian Church in Lawton. A curious life—born into a Stone Age culture, brought up to a career of rapine and slaughter, and winding up in the Atomic Age, authorship, and the sanctity of Presbyterianism.

In 1967 I happened to encounter a last remnant of the Chiricahua spirit. At the time I was a member of something called the National Advisory Commission on Rural Poverty. Its mission was to hold hearings and make studies of the hard times then endemic in the rural areas of Appalachia, the South, and the Southwest. (We came up, in due time, with a report on the causes of such poverty, and recommendations for remedying it; but President Lyndon Johnson did not like our findings and tried unsuccessfully to suppress them.)

One of our hearings was in Tucson, where we were looking into the living and working conditions of migrant farm laborers, Spanish-Americans, and Indians. Among the witnesses who appeared was a very old man, who described himself as a chief of the Chiricahua Apaches, or rather of that part of the tribe which had moved voluntarily in 1913 from Fort Sill to the Mescalero reservation in Arizona. He was dressed in Apache costume, complete with a blue headcloth. Although he understood English well enough, he insisted on testifying in his own language, with an interpreter. At considerable length he described the unhappiness of his people, although he did not exactly claim that they were living in great want.

The questioning was conducted by Congressman Herman E. Gallegos, who himself had some Indian blood. Gently and sympathetically he tried to get the witness to be specific. What precisely did he want for his people?

"A return to the old life," the chief said.

What kind of life? For nearly half an hour, the answers were vague. Then, in a burst of irritation, the old man said: "Why, of course, we just want to live as our ancestors did—on horseback, hunting and raiding the Navaho and Pueblos and Hopi."

Tactfully he did not mention such quarry as Mexicans and Arizonans.

The gist of his testimony was this: The predatory life is a happy life, so long as you can get away with it. I don't doubt it for a moment. Some of the white predators who moved into the High Plains were even more destructive in their lighthearted way than the Apaches, as we shall note in a later chapter. They were happy, too.

NINE

The Sayings

A surprising number of the early residents of the High Plains somehow found time to write about their experiences. A few, such as Charlie Siringo and Andy Adams, produced books that are still widely read. Most never got further than letters, scraps of memoirs, and memoranda about events that they considered noteworthy. But nearly all had one thing in common: they wrote bald narratives, hinting only indirectly at their feelings and views of the world. As Frank Dobie said of Siringo, he "had almost nothing to say on life; he reported actions." If you want to know something about the old-timers' values, convictions, and conclusions about the culture they lived in, you have to look to their sayings.

These remarks, or aphorisms, were occasionally recorded by someone who had heard them. But mostly they circulated by word of mouth, among people who considered them apt, for about three generations. Then, before the middle of this century, they began to die away, because they no longer applied to

123

the facts of everyday life. Even when I was a youngster, some of them had come to sound a bit cryptic.

One of the best known was the exchange between a Texas Panhandle rancher and his foreman. "If we only had water," the cattleman remarked, "this country would be a paradise." To which the foreman replied: "So would hell."

That summed up as tersely as might be the universal preoccupation with water. As the scarcest resource of the High Plains, it determined the pattern of settlement—the location of trails, the placement of ranches and of towns. It even gave the region its earliest name—the Llano Estacado, or Staked Plains. To guide future travelers, the Spanish explorers set up "stakes"—actually little piles of rocks or buffalo bones—to mark the way from one creek or playa lake to another; for if they missed one of these rare watering places, both man and horse were likely to die of thirst.*

In the Salt Fork country, where the first settlers had to haul their drinking water in barrels and grub out mesquite roots for firewood, a young housewife once spilled a bucket of water as she was climbing down from the barrel wagon. "Oh, God," she said, "how I hate a country where you have to climb for water and dig for wood."

The lust for water led to the Western adaptation of the windmill, the third technological development—after the six-shooter and barbed wire—that made the High Plains a feasible place for white people to live. Much later it also led to the deep wells, pumped by gas engines, that could tap the primeval Ogallala Aquifer and thus make possible the irrigation—temporarily—of some 6 million acres of once-arid soil. Finally it led to the damming of the Canadian River north of Amarillo, to form Lake Meredith, which now supplies the city with water and which has changed the landscape beyond the wildest imagin-

---

* As nearly as I can make out, the Spaniards meant by the Llano Estacado only that considerable part of the High Plains south of the Canadian River. But their successors often applied the term loosely to the whole region.

ings of, say, Colonel Goodnight. You can see sailboats today where jack rabbits once went thirsty.

To my generation, the sayings about Indians were more puzzling than those about water. "Never trade or race a horse with an Indian," my grandfather remarked one day while we were shucking corn. I assured him I had no thought of doing either—adding pointedly that at the moment I had no horse. "Well, when you get one," he said, "remember what I told you."

He explained no further, and it was years before I understood what he meant. When the first whites moved in, their Indian neighbors—especially the Comanches and Apaches—were by far the better judges of horse flesh, and for centuries they had delighted in the sly and prolonged rituals of dickering that lead up to a horse swap. Any Eastern farm boy who tried to bargain with them was almost certain to end up with the worst of the deal. Moreover, the Indians were master strategists in the quarter-horse racing that was a favorite pastime of both Indians and cowmen on the High Plains. Many a time a Comanche would arrive at a race meeting on a sleepy, broomtailed mustang that looked fit for nothing much except coyote bait. He would lose the first couple of heats, seeming hopelessly outclassed by the mettlesome cowboy mounts. Then, before the third heat, the Indian would bet all the money he had—perhaps all the cash assets of his entire village—at gratifying odds. When the starting gun went off this time, his horse would look like a different animal, running flat out with his belly close to the ground and his eyes bulging like the stops on an organ. As soon as he crossed the finish line, the old warrior would stuff his saddle bags with his winnings and start for home; he would not be interested in another race.

Grandpa's saying had not been rooted in prejudice, as I had half suspected, but in frontier common sense.

So, too, was his comment, "Of all the Indians, the Cherokees are the smartest and the Osages the dumbest." When oil was discovered on the Osage reservation, they become overnight the richest of the Oklahoma tribes. Soon many of them were either cheated out of their money by rascally whites or had squandered it on fancy automobiles and liquor. A hearse, with the whole family riding in the glass-enclosed coffin compartment, was a favorite Osage vehicle. One sinister gang of white predators made a practice of marrying Osage girls, then murdering them so as to inherit their headrights, which carried a share in the tribal oil money. About twenty Osages were done away with before the tribe caught on to what was happening.

The Cherokees, on the other hand, were never oil rich, but they had—and have—a native shrewdness that made them the most influential and prosperous of the Oklahoma Indians. They were the only tribe in North America that ever developed a written language, invented by a genius named Sequoya. Before they were forcibly removed from their original homeland in Georgia and neighboring states to an Oklahoma reservation, they had evolved a sophisticated civilization, including printing presses and a plantation system employing Negro slaves. I never heard of anyone who succeeded in cheating a Cherokee except President Andrew Jackson, who stole their Southeastern territories. In Oklahoma they adapted more readily than other tribes to the white culture. At least one became head of a major oil company, many are successful businessmen, and to this day it is advantageous for an Oklahoma politician to have Cherokee blood, or a Cherokee wife.

From their own experience, the Indians developed some sayings about whites. One of them I heard from an elderly Apache name Henry Whiteleather, who used to buy his groceries at a little crossroad store not far from my grandfather's farm. "Only a fool Indian," he said, "will let a white man add on him."

Years earlier it had been his custom to drive his wagon, with his wife and children, to the store about once a month to lay in a supply of flour, beans, molasses, calico, and other staples. As the family selected its goods, they stacked everything at the end of the counter. The white storekeeper would then add up the prices on the back of a paper sack, and Henry trustingly paid whatever the total came to, before toting his parcels to the wagon. One day, however, he took home with him the paper sack with the figures on it. Henry could add, too, though not so fast as the storekeeper, and when he checked over the sums that night, he discovered he had been overcharged by a couple of dollars. From then on Henry shopped on a different system. He would buy a pound of bacon, pay for it, and take it to the wagon. Then he came back for a sack of sugar, which he also paid for and stowed away—and so on, one item at a time, till he ran through his list. This method involved a lot of trudging back and forth to the wagon, but the storekeeper never again had a chance to do any addition on Henry.

The storekeeper would have been bewildered if anybody had accused him of dishonesty. Like many Oklahomans of the time, he had simply regarded Indians as fair game—as Geronimo had regarded the Mexicans. Taking advantage of Indians was, indeed, almost a matter of public policy. As early as 1830, Congress had decided to move the main Indian tribes east of the Mississippi River to Western territories, such as Kansas and Oklahoma, which at the time looked virtually worthless to whites. This decision was resisted violently by those tribes— Comanches, Kiowas, Apaches, and a few other—who already lived in the Western country and thought it belonged to them. (They had never heard of the Louisiana Purchase, and if they had they would have snorted at the idea that France had any right to sell the land they occupied.) After a good deal of bloodshed, however, the resettlement was completed shortly after the Civil War. What is now Oklahoma was divided up into reservations, each assigned to a specific tribe—except for one large tract that was not allocated to anybody. In a series of solemn treaties the Indians, both newcomers and original occupants, were assured that their reservations now belonged to them forever, and that they need not worry about any further molestation by the whites.

In practice, "forever" meant about thirty years. As the frontier of white settlement surged westward, the Oklahoma territory that had once looked worthless began to seem pretty attractive to land-hungry immigrants. Although they were legally forbidden, some of them began to filter into the Indian country to set up trading posts and stake out little farms. Occasionally indignant Indians murdered these interlopers, but others were tolerated, especially in the areas that had been allocated to the Five Civilized Tribes. These were the Cherokees, Creeks, Choctaws, Chickasaws, and Seminoles, all of whom had been forcibly removed from the Southeastern states; compared with the Plains tribes, they were relatively peaceful and sedentary people, used to farming and to rubbing elbows with white neighbors. Many of them had, in fact, fought in the Civil War, the Choctaws and Chickasaws with the Confederacy, the other three tribes with the Union armies.

Other whites wandering westward fixed their eyes on that stretch of Oklahoma land that had never been allocated to any tribe. They argued that it must still be public domain, and therefore open to white settlement. Some of them sneaked in, were evicted by soldiers, and returned as soon as the cavalry patrol was out of sight. Others organized a lobbying campaign—with the help of land speculators and the railroads, which stood to profit most from the Western migration. President Benjamin Harrison finally caved in, and proclaimed that the unallocated Oklahoma lands would be opened to settlers on April 22, 1889. The upshot was the Run—a chaotic scramble of some sixty thousand people, on foot, horse, wagon, and bicycle, bent on staking their claims before the end of the day. By sunset they had occupied what came to be six counties in the heart of the state.

Not all of the participants in the Run were heroic pioneers, as they were later portrayed in Oklahoma legend and in any number of novels and films. Many were ne'er-do-wells who had not been able to make it back East. Some were outlaws, who had been hiding out on Indian reservations where the white man's law did not reach. Others were bootleggers who had been selling illegal whiskey to the Indians, or pimps, or gamblers. A good few were cheats who had managed to slip through the cordon of U.S. troops a few days before the Run. They hid out in gulches or clumps of shinnery oaks, and then, when the starting guns were fired, they staked out choice claims before the honest contestants could get there. These characters became known as Sooners. Curiously, this was not a term of opprobrium; even the men they had cheated out of land claims usually regarded the Sooners not as scoundrels, but as clever and enterprising fellows. Eventually the word became a nickname for all Oklahomans, just as Indianians are known as Hoosiers.

The prevalance of hard cases among these settlers led to one of Colonel Goodnight's sayings, which became commonplace throughout the Texas Panhandle: "Worthless as an Oklahoman." His wife once chided him for using it, saying: "Now, Charles, you know there are lots of good people in Oklahoma."

"Damned few, Mary," he said. "Damned few."

The Run did not begin to satisfy the white appetite for Oklahoma land. Unsuccessful claimants and successive waves of immigrants from the East soon remarked that the Indians did not really need all the land within their reservations. Much of it was not even farmed, since the Indians preferred to keep it as hunting country or to lease it to white cattlemen. Besides, as the landless whites pointed out to their congressmen, Indians did not vote.

Naturally, Washington began to open up "surplus" Indian land to settlement, in installments over the fourteen years following the Run. To avoid the disorder, cheating, and claim-jumping that attended the Run, the government distributed the additional land among the many applicants by lot. It was in one of the last of these drawings, in 1903, that my father won the right to purchase the homestead near Apache—160 acres, for which he had to pay $200. The patent was signed: "By the President: T. Roosevelt."

At the time my father was a newspaper reporter on the Kansas City *Star,* earning ten dollars a week. He immediately moved to his allotted land, summoning two of his brothers, Jake and George, from Ohio to join him. With their pooled savings, they bought a plow, a mule team, and enough rough lumber to run up a house—little more than a shack. As soon as they got their first crop in, they sent for their parents, who were only too glad to sell their not-very-prosperous acreage in Ohio and start life over again among the jack rabbits and Indians of western Oklahoma. To finance the move, my father mortgaged his homestead for $800; and as soon as the old folks were well settled in, he deeded the farm to them and moved further west to try his luck in the still wilder country of the Oklahoma Panhandle.

Like many of his generation, my father was obsessed with the notion of land ownership. To him it meant not only independence, but an honorable role in the conversion of wilderness into something like civilization. His favorite saying was: "Every good citizen has a duty to own as much land as he can support." Because he really believed this, he was land-poor all his life. At one time or another he owned at least eight farms and ranches in Oklahoma, Texas, Idaho, and Oregon, including the Apache place, which reverted to him when my grandfather died. Except during his boyhood in Ohio and his brief time on the Oklahoma homestead, he never worked the land himself, preferring to rent it on shares to carefully supervised tenants. Of a good tenant, he would say: "That man works with a steady swing"—a phrase obscure to anyone who has never cut grain or hay with a scythe, as my father had done in his early years.

None of his land ever profited him much—on the contrary,

he often had to earn money in other ways to pay off his mortgages—but he left every property in better condition than when he bought it. He enjoyed managing land and was good at it. As a consequence, Eastern insurance companies commissioned him to manage and sometimes to resell farms that they had acquired through mortgage foreclosures. Following the depression of 1922 he had charge of some two hundred such properties, each one representing a personal tragedy to the family that had gone broke. Whenever possible, my father kept the former owner on as a tenant, and coached him along until he was able to repurchase the place. In almost every case, he was able to give his tenants a practical education in modern agricultural techniques, which he studied unremittingly.

One of my earliest memories is of his nightly reading. After supper he would usually read me a fairy tale or, more often, a chapter from Hurlburt's *Book of Bible Stories.* Then he would settle down to serious business—a stack of Agriculture Department bulletins and farm journals, such as *Hoard's Dairyman,* and *The Progressive Farmer,* which would occupy him far into the night. Occasionally one of his tenants would refuse to bother with the crop rotations, drought-resistant wheat seeds, or improved blood lines that my father suggested to him. A saying often attributed to such chronic failures was: "Hell, you can't tell me anything about farming. I wore out three farms while you were still a boy."

Next to farming, my father's main preoccupation was politics. He was a hereditary Republican, as my mother was a hereditary Democrat; they argued all their married life without either one ever conceding a political point to the other. "I don't claim that every Democrat is a horse thief," he would say, "but it is common knowledge that every horse thief is a Democrat." He abandoned that argument only after my mother threatened to leave him if she ever heard it again.

One of my uncles, Fletcher Fischer, used to tell a story about my father attending a hanging in Guthrie, then the territorial capital of Oklahoma. When the sheriff had adjusted the noose, he asked the condemned man if he had any last words.

"No, sheriff," he said, "At the moment I can't think of a thing to say that would do me a mite of good."

Whereupon my father—according to Fletcher—jumped onto the gallows steps and said: "In that case, will the gentleman kindly yield me his time to say a few words about the future of the Republican party in Oklahoma?"

I prefer to believe that this tale is apochryphal. But my father did become for a few years one of the younger leaders of his party; he served as secretary of the first Republican convention in the state, and later was appointed a United States land commissioner. The spirit of early Oklahoma politics was illustrated by a friend of his. When father asked him how he intended to vote, he said: "I haven't made up my mind yet, but when I do I am going to be damned bitter."

My Uncle Fletcher also dabbled in politics—he once ran a hopeless race for the governorship of Texas—but his chief interests were ranching and the practice of law. Like all my other relatives, he advised me freely on the conduct of my life, but since he was the earthiest of the lot—a domineering, rough-spoken man of large appetites—his counsel had a more worldly tone. Here are three rules that he assured me would be unfailingly serviceable:

1. Never draw to an inside straight, and always check to the one-card draw.
2. Never trust a cow with white eyelashes, a walleyed horse, or a woman with black underwear.
3. When you ride into town, always stop just before you get there to piss and count your money.

The rules that Uncle Bob Baxter bequeathed to me were less sophisticated but, I found, equally reliable.

"As a matter of common courtesy," he said, "never ask a man

where he comes from. If he's from Texas, he will let you know. If not, don't embarrass him."

He also cautioned me: "Always check the cinch before you get on a horse. The old bastard probably puffed up on you." What he meant was that many a range horse had a habit of puffing out his belly while you were saddling and cinching him. By the time you got the bridle on and were ready to mount, he would have relaxed so that the cinch might be dangerously loose. Hence it was prudent to run a finger under the girth, and if necessary tighten it up a notch or two before stepping into the stirrup.

His attitude toward government—any government—was summed up by his comment on Charles P. Garlock after that one-time cattleman took a job with the Department of Agriculture: "I guess he had to. I heard his health was failing."

And his view of bankers, as illustrated by a remark about the president of an Amarillo bank: "If you ever have to shake hands with Mr. Fuqua, count your fingers."

Of farmers, too, Mr. Baxter was mildly contemptuous, although in his later years he raised a little cotton and milo maize* on his own Shamrock ranch. Wheat farmers, in particular, he regarded as a lazy bunch. Dry-land winter wheat can be raised—if enough rain comes at the right time—with at most ten to twenty weeks of work a year. After that, the wheat farmer can devote the rest of his time to other occupations, or to the finer things of life. A good many of them, alas, spent a lot of this spare time loafing around the small towns of the Panhandle. As Mr. Baxter and I drove through Shamrock one afternoon, he called my attention to the local domino parlor. "If lightning hit that building right now," he said, "it would kill half the wheat farmers in Wheeler County."

---

*The popular strain of maize at that time was Hegira, an import from the Middle East, presumably named after the flight of the Prophet Mohammed from Mecca to Medina; in north Texas it was quickly corrupted into "High Gear."

He disapproved even more strongly of people who hunted for sport. "Never kill anything you don't mean to eat" was an injunction he drilled into Robert and me at every opportunity; and I have observed it ever since. He made an exception for rattlesnakes, coyotes (which sometimes kill lambs and calves), and jack rabbits, which can do a lot of damage to a grain or hay crop. But he scolded Robert and me for a rabbit-hunting game we invented during one teen-age summer when we bought, jointly, a stripped-down Model T Ford for fifteen dollars.

It is a peculiarity of rabbits that if they are caught at night by the headlights of a car, they will run straight ahead in the beam, rather than dodging off to one side. So soon after dark, Robert and I would set out across the prairie, one of us driving and the other sitting on the right front fender with a 22-caliber pistol. When we started a rabbit, the boy with the gun would pop away until he hit the animal running in the beam—or, more often, emptied all six chambers without a hit, since accurate shooting was difficult from a light car jouncing over sagebrush and bunch-grass hummocks. Then we would change places and try again. Mr. Baxter did all he could to discourage these safaris—partly because he was afraid that we might wreck our jalopy, or fall off and break an arm, or shoot a tire or each other by accident. But he also disapproved, I suspect, because he thought we enjoyed it too much; next thing he knew, we might turn into sportsmen.

When Mr. Baxter did approve of someone, wholeheartedly and without reservation, he was likely to say: "He will do to ride the river with." The river he had in mind was the Salt Fork or maybe the Canadian, but other old-timers who used the same phrase might have been thinking about the Nueces or Brazos or Rio Grande. Twice a year, before the spring and fall roundups, cow hands went out in pairs to comb the river banks for cattle that might be hiding in the brush and cottonwood groves. It was always an arduous chore, and in the earliest days a dangerous one, since a band of cattle thieves or irritable Comanches might be encountered around the next bend. A good partner for riding the river had to be reliable, skilled in his profession, resourceful in emergencies, courageous against any odds, willing to do his share of the work or more, and preferably—though not necessarily—agreeable company around a campfire for weeks on end. Not many men qualified, at least in Mr. Baxter's view.

One who must have was buried near the Salt Fork on the old Rocking Chair range. His headstone had been a plank from a wagon box, on which his fellow cowboys had burned an epitaph. Both grave and plank had disappeared long before my time, but Mr. Baxter told me about them. The inscription had read: "Sammy done his damnedest. Angels can do no more."

TEN

Growing Up on the Salt Fork

One of the more bitter sayings among High Plains people was: "Texas is a fine place for men and dogs, but hell on women and horses." It did not apply, however, to the Caperton girls. By their own testimony, all five of them found the Panhandle a rugged but satisfying place to grow up.

For the earliest women in that country, the most hellish aspect of life was loneliness. Many of them, like Mary Goodnight when she made her home at the JA ranch, lived at least two days' ride from any feminine company. What male companionship they had was hardly scintillating; the men came to headquarters only to eat, sleep, and change horses, and their conversation dealt almost exclusively with livestock and the weather. A traveling cowboy with gossip from the outside world, and perhaps an old newspaper, was a welcome surprise, but a rare one. A visit with another woman was a treat that could be expected only a few times a year.

But from the beginning the Caperton women were more fortunate. Because the two Caperton families had migrated together, and built dugouts within sight of each other, the sharing of labor and company was an almost daily occurrence. Within a year of their arrival on the Salt Fork, other homesteaders had settled near enough so that a housewife could load a wagon full of her youngsters, drive to the Capertons for lunch, and still get home before dark.

The neighborhood plainly needed a school, so the men built one—a single-room planked shack with wooden benches, a potbellied stove, and a blackboard. They imported a teacher from Wellington, a tiny settlement that had grown up around the Rocking Chair headquarters. She was a slender, lovely eighteen-year-old girl named Seigniora Russell—Nonie for short—well qualified for teaching because her father (then a farmer) had once been a superintendent of schools in Arkansas, and had tutored her diligently at home. Her salary was twenty-seven dollars a month, good pay at a time when top cow hands got thirty.

Since all but four of her thirteen pupils were Capertons, she was, naturally, quartered in one of the George Caperton dugouts. Each morning she walked the mile or so to her schoolhouse with her brood surrounding her like a flock of chickens. She later wrote, in her autobiography, *Sand in My Eyes,** that "there was little, if any, pupil-teacher distinction. We were really a group of children working together. Discipline, as such, was unknown. We all played together at recess and studied hard during the school hours." For the rest of her life she remained an honorary Caperton; I was half grown before I realized that she and her children were not, in fact, blood relatives.

* Philadelphia: Lippincott, 1956.

The ultimate safeguard against loneliness was the post office. Once a week, weather and ranch duties permitting, a Rocking Chair cowboy rode the twenty miles from Wellington with a sack of mail for the families living near Dozier Creek; and at the request of her neighbors, Mary Helen Caperton served as their local postmistress. Her equipment was a packing box nailed to the wall, with a pigeonhole for each of the families in the district. In her autobiography, Seigniora Russell Laune wrote:

> To the Caperton dugout the people came, ostensibly, to get their mail. On Sundays, especially, the yard around the dugout was filled with horses and vehicles as though some sort of celebration were being held. Wagons drew up, spilling out children in their Sunday best, with lean, work-worn fathers in clean shirts and faded Levis, and tired-eyed mothers wearing crisp, ruffled sun bonnets and starched aprons. Young men who worked the range . . . swung from their horses that were left "ground hitched."* Sometimes a young man self-consciously brought his girl in a buggy, which was pure affectation as all girls rode horseback.
>
> The women crowded together in the kitchen while the older men sat on the corral fence or on the wagon tongues, for man-talk of cattle and crops. The young men and girls clustered around the piano in the living-bedroom. Everybody sang while the older people ate at first table. Then came the hungry second table of young people called from their music; then the children, squirming and pushing, who had been fortified, but in no way satisfied, with bread-'n'butter'n-jelly. How in the world Mrs. Caperton managed, even with the help of her young daughters, and the very questionable help of her visitors, to feed the hungry horde that swarmed around her table month after month, is now a mystery to me. At the time, I am afraid, we took her hospitality for granted as a custom of the times and place. . . .
>
> In the evening during the week, the nesters, the ranchers, and I gathered in the dugout to hear Mrs. Caperton read. We sat on the steps that led down from the outside into the room, on the chairs, on the big puffy beds that were curtained off for sleeping, and on the

---

* Cow ponies were trained to stand still when their bridle reins were left trailing on the ground—a necessity in open country, where hitching posts and trees were few and far between.

floor leaning against the walls. She read first the newspapers, days old; then the magazines, often slipped from their wrappers and carefully returned to the compartment in the post office marked with the name of the subscriber; or she read a chapter from *Pilgrim's Progress, Vanity Fair,* or one of Dickens' novels. These old classics were new to many of her listeners, and she wanted her children to become familiar with them.

After the reading and the talk, the older people would take their mail and ride over the long miles of moon-and-star-lit prairie to their homes. The baby in Mrs. Caperton's arms, and the other little children who had found willing laps in which to cuddle during the reading, were gathered up and put to bed. The furniture was pushed back and those who remained square danced, while Mrs. Caperton played the piano.

So much for the notion that rural life of the last century, even on the High Plains, was invariably lonesome.

For learning beyond what Nonie Russell could offer, the girls went to "summer normal schools" in Wellington, and occasionally had a private tutor. The older boys took jobs as cowboys and, as soon as they became of age, homesteaded land of their own. My mother, Georgie Caperton, the youngest of the daughters, got the most education, because by the time she was fifteen the family was prosperous enough to send her for four years to a boarding school, Goodnight College. The first venture into higher learning in the Texas Panhandle, it was founded by Colonel Goodnight and his wife in 1898 with $30,000 of their own money, simply because they believed the country needed such an institution—and because it had long been the Colonel's habit to take the lead in anything that interested him, from law enforcement to crossbreeding cattle. He had a substantial brick and sandstone building put up in the little town of Goodnight, a whistle stop on the Fort Worth & Denver Railway, where the old man had established his last ranch. (It was a mere 160 square miles in size, a small enterprise compared with his old empire on the JA range.) Goodnight himself served as president of the college's board of directors, and handled the business management. To head the faculty, he imported Marshal McIllhany, a scholar who had reputedly been educated at Harvard. The staff probably never came to more than half a dozen teachers, but—to judge from their corrections on the essays and exercise books I found among my mother's papers—they were both competent and rigorous. The courses they offered were English literature, mathematics, Spanish, history, and elementary bookkeeping; and the level of instruction apparently was about equal to that of most junior colleges today. In one respect it was superior: Goodnight graduates all had to be able to write clear, coherent English with correct spelling and grammar—an accomplishment by no means universal among more recent college graduates.

The students paid what tuition they could, often in beef and hides, and the boys—who usually commuted on horseback—tended a small garden, orchard, and dairy herd on the back lot. The girls lived in and helped pay their way by doing the housekeeping. On at least one occasion the whole student body, together with the faculty and the Goodnight ranch hands, had to turn out with wet brooms and gunnysacks to fight a prairie fire that threatened to wipe the place out. To hear my mother tell it, the college operated much like a modern commune. Complete equality of the sexes, in both rights and responsibilities, was taken for granted—although sexual permissiveness was of course unheard of, like drugs and liquor on campus. Undergraduates never dreamed of rebelling against the Establishment, because, barring a windmill and a barbed-wire fence, there wasn't any, as far as the eye could reach. Their role was to learn to found some kind of establishment in an all-but-empty landscape.

The college survived for only about ten years, because there was not enough money on the Panhandle to support it—although Colonel Goodnight continued to pour his own resources into it, and levied contributions on the more prosperous of the neighboring ranchers. The last time I passed that way the only trace of it was a heap of rubble among some overgrown shrubbery half a mile north of U.S. 287. But while it lasted, it did make a memorable contribution to what passed for civilization on the High Plains.

For Georgie Caperton, the college opened a door to a career as a teacher and independent homesteader. Soon after her graduation in 1903, she paid an extended visit to her older sister Evelyn, who, after her marriage to Joe Williams—for years the favorite cowboy of the whole Dozier community—had moved with him to Texhoma, a miniscule town that straddled the Texas-Oklahoma border about 150 miles northwest of the Caperton ranch; there Joe had launched a ranching venture of his own. At the Williamses' suggestion Georgie applied for the teacher's job in the Texhoma school, a one-room enterprise much like the one Nonie Russell had taught on the Salt Fork. After a brief interview, the school board hired her, with a warning that she might have some disciplinary problems, since none of her pupils had ever attended school, some were nearly as old as she was, and a few of the boys were a good deal bigger.

The first morning she did have, as she put it, "a little difficulty." The biggest boy—one of the numerous McMurtry clan—refused her request that he stoke up the stove. She picked up a chunk of firewood from the wood box and knocked him down. When he got up spluttering and waving his arms, she knocked him down again. From then on there was no doubt about who was forewoman in that schoolroom, and she had no further problems that she could not handle with a cottonwood switch.

I once asked her whether her pupils ever complained to their parents about her disciplinary methods.

"Of course not," she said, "If they had, they knew they would get a worse switching at home."

Incidentally, Joe Williams' sister eventually married a McMurtry. Her grandson, Larry McMurtry, has become one of the most reliable writers about contemporary life in north Texas. His *Horseman, Pass By,* made into a film and paperback under the title of *Hud,* is the best recent novel I know of about ranch life; and his pieces published in *Harper's* in 1968 and 1970 are notable for their meticulous, if sometimes painful, accuracy.

Following another of Joe Williams' suggestions, Georgie decided to homestead a piece of land of her own. She chose a tract on the Oklahoma side of the line, where the land laws were slightly more advantageous than those of Texas. Anyone could file a claim on 160 acres of unoccupied land owned by the federal government. The claimant was supposed to build a house, plant a crop, and live on the property for at least a year; after meeting these requirements to the satisfaction of the local U.S. land commissioner, the homesteader could get final title by paying $1.25 an acre. In practice, nobody took the rules too seriously. They had been designed originally for the fertile and well-watered soils of the Midwest, where 160 acres was enough for a good family-sized farm. On the High Plains, before irrigation became possible, no crop was dependable except the native grasses, and no family could hope to live on a mere quarter-section. It was generally understood that as soon as a homesteader had proved up his claim, he would abandon his house and token crop—usually a few acres of forlorn maize or sorghum—and then sell or lease the land to a neighboring rancher who needed more pasture.

Accompanied by the Williamses, Georgie went to the Texhoma land office to file her claim. There Joe introduced her to "my old friend, Commissioner Fischer." To her, he seemed an imposing personage—younger than she had expected, but dressed in a black suit with a necktie and a gates-ajar celluloid wing collar. He sat behind a shiny oak desk, piled high with important-looking papers, and with a derby hat on one corner. He greeted her solemnly, shook hands, and assured her he would do all he could to help with her claim. (Only weeks later did she learn that the scene had been prearranged by Joe and Mr. Fischer for her benefit; normally the commissioner worked in his shirt sleeves like everybody else, and saved his frock coat and derby for funerals and political rallies.)

John S. Fischer had been granted the commissionership as a reward for his services to the Republican party. It was not an arduous job, so he had little trouble running a weekly newspaper, the Texhoma *Times,* in his spare time, with the help of an elderly tramp printer. Mr. Fischer wrote all the news stories and editorials, sold advertising, solicited subscriptions, and handset much of the type; in fact, he composed much of his copy at the type cases, without bothering to write it out in longhand first. He had learned the country editor's profession on his own, by putting out two even smaller weeklies in Beaver City and Carnegie, Oklahoma, immediately after he had moved west from the Apache homestead.

As commissioner, he was supposed to visit all the homesteaders in his district from time to time, to see whether they were complying with the residence and farming rules—a duty that fitted neatly with his editor's chore of collecting local news items. It may have been that he visited Georgie Caperton's shanty somewhat oftener than was strictly necessary.

She actually did live on her claim a good part of the time, in the one-room shelter that Joe Williams had run up for her, although she usually spent at least weekends at the Williamses' place. Her farming was pretty much limited to a vegetable garden, a patch of maize, and a few flowers. For her daily trip to and from school, six miles each way, she had Little Blue, an elderly retired cow pony.

Didn't a girl ever get scared under such circumstances?

"Yes," she said, "I got real scared once. I was about halfway to school one morning when a hailstorm broke. Some of the hailstones were nearly as big as baseballs, and if one of them hit me, I was pretty sure it would crack my skull. So I took the saddle off Little Blue, held it over my head, and ran the rest of the way to the schoolhouse."

What happened to the horse, I asked.

"Oh, he got a few lumps, but the hailstones didn't really hurt him. His old head was too thick."

She was never sentimental about horses, and to my knowledge never got aboard one except when necessary. Riding as a sport never occurred to her, for the same reason that truck drivers don't go pleasure-driving on Sunday mornings.

I suspect that her memory exaggerated the size of those hailstones. In that same country, however, I have seen them the size of golf balls, pelting down with force enough to dent car tops and knock the shingles off houses, so her fright was not just a case of girlish hysteria.

Within a year after her arrival in Texhoma Georgie and Mr. Fischer (as she called him all her life) became engaged. I don't think he ever knew—as I did not, until several years after his death—that she was already engaged to four other young men. As she saw it, no girl could have an oversupply of potential husbands, although she need not be hasty in deciding finally which one to keep. Now she made up her mind: Mr. Fischer had a promising business, sober habits, a religious upbringing, and a better education than any of her other fiancés (mostly self-acquired, since he had only a few years of formal education in rural Ohio schools). He was a veteran of the Spanish-American War, and a respected public official. Moreover, he was almost the first man she had ever met who did not have to make his living on horseback, or keeping store—certainly the first who owned a derby hat. Besides, they were devoted to each other. They married in 1908, and I don't think either of them ever regretted it.

Georgie must have disposed of her other young men with reasonable tact, because one of them, H. Otis Bynum, remained a lifelong friend and a welcome companion during her twenty years of widowhood.

Soon after their engagement, Mr. Fischer had a home built for them—a bleak place, from the only snapshot of it that I have. But both of my parents assured me that it was one of the better houses in Texhoma at that time. Although it had only four rooms, it was painted white and equipped with a fence, lightning rods, and a storm cellar where they could take refuge from the tornadoes that often ravage the High Plains. There they lived for four years, until they decided (correctly) that Texhoma's future was limited. Then they moved on, as Western settlers so often did—to Salt Lake City, Boise, Idaho, and eventually to Amarillo. When I tried many years later to locate their first home, it had disappeared, and nobody in Texhoma could identify its site. So I have never known, for sure, whether I was born in Oklahoma or Texas.

Until she died in 1971, at the age of eighty-seven, Georgie Fischer held strong opinions on every conceivable subject except one. The women's liberation movement baffled her. She could never figure out what it was all about, since she had never felt oppressed for a moment in her life. The idea that other women might feel the need to rear and whinny against male domination was simply beyond her grasp. Her attitude toward men was one of wary affection, like that of a lion tamer toward her performing cats. If she did not watch them carefully, they might try to get out of hand, but it was then her duty to put them, firmly and kindly, back into their places; and she never had the faintest doubt that she could do it. If she got clawed now and then, well, that was just the nature of the beasts, and she did not resent them for it.

For Grandmother Caperton had raised all her daughters to be experienced managers of men. Because she was too busy running the household to pay much attention to the younger children, she handed that responsibility over to her daughters as soon as they were old enough to change a diaper. Georgie's special charges were the two youngest sons, Albert and Kenneth, both of whom she adored. After licking them into shape from infancy to adolescence, she never lacked confidence in her ability to handle anything else in trousers.

Before her marriage, Georgie asked Mr. Fischer to promise that he would never take another drink—a pledge he kept with no strain, since he, too, had been raised in a strict Methodist family. Even in his relatively carefree bachelor days he had never drunk anything more than an occasional glass of beer at a political meeting. His reputation for sobriety helped reconcile her family to the marriage—although George Caperton could never quite forgive his daughter for marrying a Yankee.

In addition to protecting the men under their jurisdiction from the evils of drink, the Caperton women considered themselves guardians against sin in all its other guises, notably gambling and wastrel habits. Consequently, my father never touched a card or bet on a horse; but his wife could never quite manage to suppress his inclination to speculate in land and livestock, which he insisted was investment, not gambling. As a result, on two occasions—the depressions of 1920 and 1932—he lost nearly everything and found himself deeply in debt. These disasters reinforced my mother's conviction that frugality was a cardinal virtue. She cut down my father's old suits to make clothes for me and my brother, saved his worn ties to make piece quilts, and cooked on a wood range long after most of our neighbors had shifted to gas or electric stoves.

Even in her old age, when she didn't really need to be so thrifty, she insisted on keeping scraps of leftover food that any other housewife would have tossed into the garbage pail; and I don't think she ever took a taxi without a twinge of guilt.

Regular churchgoing was, of course, regarded as a prophylaxis against sin. My mother saw to it, therefore, that the whole family went to Sunday school and two services on Sunday and usually to a prayer meeting or church supper in midweek. She also took us to hear every traveling evangelist who came to town and enrolled me early in the Epworth League, the Methodist equivalent of Hitler's *Jugend*. The upshot of this enforced piety was that I felt, when I was old enough to leave home, that I had heard enough sermons for one lifetime. I have avoided churches with considerable success ever since.

Among her maxims for the governance of men, one of my mother's favorites was: "The devil finds mischief for idle hands to do." My brother and I were saved from idleness, so far as she could help it, from the time we were big enough to make ourselves useful. At the age of six, for example, my list of chores included taking care of a pen of chickens—smelly, addlebrained creatures that I loathed. Most Sundays, moreover, I had to catch a rooster, chop off his head, and clean and pluck him for dinner—an assignment I loathed even more, since a determined rooster is a fairly even match for a small boy. To this day I have no appetite for chicken in any form.

The anti-idleness program also included such jobs as chopping firewood, stoking and cleaning the furnace, mowing lawns, peddling comb honey from door to door, and selling the *Saturday Evening Post*. For the household chores I got no allowance—Mother did not hold with such foolishness—but I did keep anything I earned from outside enterprises. I was encouraged, however, to set aside a tenth of these earnings for Sunday school collection, and to salt away at least half of what was left in a savings account, against the day I might go to college.

All of this, I am afraid, sounds a little grim—which would be misleading. Like all small boys, I developed a substantial talent for passive resistance, thus defeating many of my mother's schemes to lead me into the paths of industry and righteousness. She gave up on piano lessons, for instance, before I was ten, and most days I contrived to spend more hours at play than at work. Besides, for all her determination, she did not have a grim bone in her body. She loved gaiety of all kinds—at least those that didn't cost money—and was forever organizing picnics, fishing trips, taffy pulls, and hayrides. She also loved to dance (as my father, alas, did not) and one of her abiding sorrows was that neither she nor anybody else could teach me to waltz. A boy who could not waltz, she felt, was as ill educated as one who could not ride, shoot, fish, swim, or handle an ax.

She disapproved of fighting, but she disapproved even more of my getting licked. When I came home from school one day, bloody and blubbering, at about the age of seven, she insisted that my father give me boxing lessons. Though she did not know it, he was nearly as unskilled in that art as I was; but he dutifully bought boxing gloves for both of us and sparred with me in the backyard until he thought I was passably nimble. I must have learned something, because I seemed to hold my own at recess from then on; and when I finally did get to college I was able to earn part of my expenses by boxing occasionally in welterweight matches at American Legion and Elks Club smokers.

In public life, as at home, my mother believed that women were divinely appointed to serve as custodians of morals. She worked hard for the Women's Christian Temperance Union and for its main cause, prohibition; and she was an early, enthusiastic advocate of women's suffrage. At an age when I could barely count pennies, much less understand the Gold

Question, she took me to a chautauqua lecture by William Jennings Bryan, who was as interminable as he was illustrious. When I began, after the first hour or two, to squirm and whine, she told me to hush up.

"Never mind if you can't understand the words," she said. "He's a great Democrat and you should be edified to be here."

I wasn't—but again I learned something. When I was asked, many years later, to help write speeches for Democratic presidential candidates, I kept them short and avoided the Gold Question.

One of her more original political notions was that all bachelors should be heavily taxed. The Christian duty of every man, she believed, was to marry early, raise a family, and support it as best he could. Any shirker manifestly should be made to feel the teeth of the public fisc. Sometimes, usually after she had been condoling with an old maid, she went further.

"An old bachelor," she would proclaim, "is the meanest thing in the world. If I had my way, I would shoot them all."

Until she was a very old woman, she never heard of homosexuality, and then she did not believe it.

If she had lived to discuss the women's liberation movement with Betty Friedan or Gloria Steinem, she would, I am sure—well, fairly sure—have tried her best to be gentle and understanding. She realized that she had grown up with advantages no longer available to them, and perhaps never again to any but a negligible number of American women—notably an early chance to sprout confidence and self-reliance under the best of growing conditions. She would have sympathized, too, with women's lib in its complaints about the current crop of young men, whom she considered mostly a sorry lot—lazy, uncurried, rarely harness broken, and unschooled in the deference she felt they owed to the more responsible sex. But she also believed that these failings were largely the fault of today's women, who had neglected to enforce Decent Standards; and for the whining self-pity that seems to affect a good many lib types, she would have had no patience whatever. Nor, indeed, any comprehension.

"What do they want to be liberated *from?*" she once asked me.

"Well, men, I guess."

"Fiddlesticks!"

ELEVEN

Oil

The first oil rig I ever saw was drilling in Mr. Baxter's pasture near Shamrock. It was the venture of a Mr. Schenck, a wildcat oil operator from New York, who had raised the money and hired the drilling crew. If I understood the business arrangements correctly, he had leased the mineral rights from Mr. Baxter for a modest down payment and a promise of 10 percent royalties on any oil and gas that he might find. He boarded at the Baxter home, where I also was living at the time, and he soon became a sort of hero to both Robert Baxter and me. He was plump, good-natured, and percolating with optimism—a necessary character trait for a wildcatter—and he was the only urbane character we had ever seen. Mr. Schenck wore a Palm Beach suit, a Panama hat, and a bow tie, all sartorial novelties in the Panhandle of the twenties. In the evenings he would tell us stories about Broadway and Wall Street and ocean liners and other wonders, and he used the long-distance telephone lines with an insouciance that made us think he was a millionaire, which he certainly was not; at the time he probably was living on borrowed money.

The rig was worked by a crew of roughnecks who camped at the site. "Roughneck" is not a derogatory term. It is the traditional title for practitioners of a skilled, difficult, and dangerous profession, and a highly paid one. They were sweaty, taciturn men in overalls who chewed tobacco—smoking around a potential gas well is imprudent—and swore nonstop in a level and resigned tone of voice. They expected trouble at any moment, and they usually got it.

They were working what was known as a "standard" rig, now a museum item if any still exists. Its main feature was a slender pyramidal wooden derrick, which suspended a bit and string of weights on a wire cable that ran down into the well. A big steam-driven wheel near the foot of the derrick would lift the string of tools about ten feet above the bottom of the hole and then a few seconds later drop it with an earth-shaking thump. Each impact of the bit—which might be fish-tailed or some other shape, depending on the geological formation—would pulverize a few handfuls of rock. From time to time the bit would be pulled out and replaced by another tool that could scoop and remove the powdered rock, or sometimes mud when a vein of water was seeping into the hole. If the rig was drilling through dolomite limestone, or sand, it might go down several feet a day. Harder formations took longer, and the almost daily accidents caused further expensive delays.

The most frequent mishap was the loss of the bit. The cable might break, or the hole might begin to go crooked when it reached a hard, slanting layer of rock, thus jamming the bit. Then a specialized tool, something like giant sugar tongs, had to be lowered into the well to grapple and lift out the lost bit and piece of cable—a process of blind fishing that might take days.

Accidents of a dozen other kinds could happen, and often did. A roughneck could get an arm or foot crushed while the crew was lifting lengths of pipe to be lowered into the well as lining; or the crown block at the top of the derrick could jam; or, on rare occasions, the bit could unexpectedly tap an underground reservoir of gas or oil, which might then gush upwards with explosive force. A really big gusher might hurl the bit out of the hole and destroy the derrick, along with anyone working on it at the time. I once saw such an explosive gusher, the day after it blew, near Oklahoma City. It was called I.T.I.O. No. 1 Mary Sudik—that is, the company putting down the hole was the Indian Territory Illuminating Oil Company, and the well was its first on the property it had leased from Mrs. Sudik. The well shot a roaring plume of oil and gas hundreds of feet into the air, covering the earth with oil to a depth of about three inches for several miles around. As a reporter for the *Oklahoma Daily,* I was permitted to approach within half a mile, a rough safety limit decreed by the county sheriff, in case a spark should set the well on fire. If that had happened, the oil-drenched crew struggling to cap the well with a Christmas tree valve* would have been cremated in seconds.

No oil, alas, ever gushed from Mr. Schenck's well. Before he got down to five thousand feet—a respectable depth for a standard rig—he ran out of hope, or money, or both, and arranged to have the rig hauled off to a more promising site. Some of my Wheeler County kinfolk did eventually make money out of oil and gas, but more from acting as lease brokers than from royalties on their own land. Despite my father's slow-dying hopes, no well was ever drilled on any Fischer property.

* So called because it was a heavy steel cone, open at the bottom, with many steel valves projecting from its sides, something like the branches of a Christmas tree. The problem was to lower this cone over the wellhead, fasten it securely, and then close the valves one by one until the flow was shut off. As I remember it, the choking down of "Wild Mary" took more than a week. Providentially, she never caught fire.

The standard rig technique would look pathetically primitive to anyone who has ever watched a modern rotary drill. Its bit grinds away at the end of a rotating pipe; not only is it much faster than the old standard rig, but it can reach far greater depths, operate below the surface of the sea, and can angle holes in any direction, as well as straight down. Often several shafts are driven from a single drilling platform. Incidentally, Howard Hughes' fortune was originally based on an ingenious and uniquely efficient rotary bit developed by his father and marketed along with other drilling equipment by the Hughes Tool Company.

The father of the oil and gas industry on the High Plains was Charles N. Gould, a geology professor at the University of Oklahoma. He was commissioned by Theodore Roosevelt to make a survey of water resources in the drainage basin of the Canadian River. Consequently, he roamed over much of the Texas Panhandle on foot, horseback, and covered wagon for three years, from 1903 to 1905, making detailed notes on the geology of the region. One peculiarity he noted was an anticline running roughly parallel with the Canadian. By observing the dip, or slant, of rock strata visible on the surface, he concluded that eons ago the wrinkling of the earth's crust had pushed up all of the underlying layers of rock and sand into a long hump, roughly the shape of a Roman barrel arch. (You can get the same effect by bending a magazine so that both its spine and its open edge rest on your coffee table; each of its leaves would then represent a separate geological stratum.)

He also noted domelike formations underlying the flat prairie, undetectable to anyone without some knowledge of geology. One of these was near the ancient Alibates flint quarries mentioned in Chapter 2. Gould deduced the presence of a dome from the slanting surface layer of a peculiar white limestone, which he named "Alibates dolomite."

The young geologist knew that if oil and gas were present underground, they would tend to migrate upward through tilted layers of sand and porous rock to the top of the dome or anticline, and were likely to be trapped there by upper strata of harder, less permeable rock, such as slate. He had been hired to study water, not oil, however; and after he filed his report with the government, he "promptly proceeded to forget about the whole thing."*

Ten years later, Gould had two visitors from Amarillo— M. C. Nobles, a wholesale grocer, and T. J. Moore, one of his salesmen. They told him they were interested in oil possibilities, and asked whether he could suggest any promising drilling sites in the Texas Panhandle. Gould could. Remembering the domes and anticlines he had observed near the Canadian River, he offered to guide them to the telltale outcropping of Alibates dolomite.

After a field reconnaissance with Gould, the two grocerymen and a few of their friends began to buy oil and gas leases on both sides of the Canadian until they controlled about 70,000 acres, mostly within the boundaries of the Bivins and Masterson ranches. They formed the Amarillo Oil Company, and engaged the Hapgood drilling firm of Oklahoma City to put down an exploratory well for them at a site suggested by Gould. The historic Hapgood No. 1 Masterson was started—or "spudded in" as oilmen say—in December of 1917. A year and about $70,000 later it hit gas, and plenty of it; this discovery well eventually proved capable of producing 10 million cubic feet a day. But to the disappointment of the investors, they got no oil. At the time, gas seemed virtually worthless, since there were no pipelines to take it to potential markets.

Other oil companies consulted Gould, and in 1921 the first oil began to flow from the Canadian River formations he had

* As recorded in Gould's memoirs, *Covered Wagon Geologist* (Norman: University of Oklahoma Press, 1959).

discovered, out of a well known as Gulf No. 2 Burnett about three miles southwest of the present site of Borger, Texas. Again, it was a disappointment. Production came to little more than two hundred barrels a day, and it was of poor quality, so heavy that it congealed into a waxy gel at normal temperatures. During the next few years about twenty other producing wells were drilled with indifferent success. Altogether they flowed less than three thousand barrels of oil a day, which was collected by a primitive little pipeline system that took it to the town of Panhandle for shipment to distant markets by railway tank cars.

The really big action started only in 1926, with two crucial events. The Dixon Creek Oil Company brought in a sure-enough producer—more than a thousand barrels a day—in the Borger area, and Humble Oil Company built a ten-inch pipeline to carry the oil all the way to the Gulf Coast. As a result, the town of Borger sprang into life literally overnight. Within six months it had a population of 35,000 and before the year was over some 800 wells were pouring out more than 160,000 barrels a day.

Only a minority of Borger's residents were oil workers. The rest were bootleggers, gamblers, dope pushers, prostitutes, thieves, land speculators, and a variety of other hustlers who swarmed in like flies to a beef carcass. They lived in tents and hastily thrown-up shacks and adobes, scattered at random among the oil derricks. The boom town did not even have a road. All its supplies, including thousands of tons of pipe and drilling equipment, had to come in by truck over the naked prairie from Amarillo, more than thirty miles away. When the track became too rutted, the next truck driver started another one a few yards to the left or right, until the sagebrush and buffalo grass was torn up over a strip about half a mile wide. Both sides of this strip were lined with broken-down vehicles. A cloud of dust hung over it all summer, and winter rains turned it into an axle-deep morass.

The settlement at the end of these tracks was both noisy and malodorous. The thump of the oil rigs and the grunt of straining trucks went on day and night. The bars and gambling joints—estimated at more than eight hundred—seldom closed. You could smell Borger at least a mile before you reached it—a stench compounded of exhaust fumes, dust, thousands of improvised privies, and the vapor from the sump pits, great holes filled with overspilled crude oil.

For the first three years of its existence, Borger made Tascosa, in its wildest days, look like a Baptist prayer meeting. There was no effective government; the town was dominated by its criminals. On payday roughnecks were often robbed on the street before they could get to the nearest saloon. More than twenty murders were reported in that period, and innumerable others went unreported. It was easy to shove a body into a sump pit, and if it was ever found—which was unlikely—nobody could tell whether it had belonged to a murder victim or to a drunk who had stumbled in at night. The few law officers present could often be intimidated or bribed—whores paid eighteen dollars a week in protection money—and those who could not be were walking targets. Two of the latter were deputy sheriffs, Patrick Kenyon and Elmer Terry. When both were gunned down on the same day, the Hutchinson County sheriff had to admit that he needed outside help. He wired Gov. Dan Moody to request a detachment of Rangers.

Ten of them arrived on April 7, 1927, and promptly started to clean up the town. In those days Rangers were little more concerned with the niceties of due process and the legal rights of the criminal than they had been when they were fighting Comanches. When they found a still they chopped it up. When they came on a cache of illegal whiskey, usually in half-gallon jars, they smashed it on the spot. In one night they confiscated more than a hundred gambling outfits, from slot machines to roulette tables, and peremptorily told the operators to get out of town. They had the same news for the prostitutes. Within twenty-four hours of the Rangers' arrival, some twelve hundred women were on the trail to Amarillo, the only way out. Those who could hitched rides with truck drivers. The others trudged through the dust, swearing with every step. A law officer who witnessed this exodus later told me, doubled up with laughter, that he had seen one lady stumbling across the plains wearing nothing except high-heeled slippers and a mink coat.

The criminal element did not give up without a fight. One of the Rangers was Frank Hamer, who years later ended the career of Clyde Barrow and who was grossly libeled in the recent film, *Bonnie and Clyde*. (Nobody ever took a gun away from Frank Hamer, as one sequence in that film would have us believe.) One noontime, as he stepped out of a corner café, he was ambushed by four men who were waiting in each of the streets leading to the intersection. They started shooting as soon as he came through the door, from four different directions, but they must have been a little nervous. None of them even grazed him. Hamer got them all with four shots, although accounts differ as to how many were killed and how many wounded.

Soon after, a traveling salesman from Chicago hit town with a sample case full of bulletproof vests, which he thought should become a fashionable item in the oil fields. He accosted a Ranger who was having dinner in a flyblown little eatery, and unpacked his wares. The Ranger resisted the sales pitch courteously, explaining that a canvas vest lined with laminated steel plates would be too hot and heavy, and that in any case he did not feel the need for such finery. The salesman persisted until the Ranger—already a little bilious from a bad meal—lost patience.

"You say your product is guaranteed?" the Ranger asked.

"Yes, indeed, fully guaranteed by one of the most reliable hardware firms in Chicago."

"You are sure about that?"

"Absolutely."

"All right," the Ranger said, drawing his gun, "put on that vest."

The salesman paled, swallowed hard, and launched into a heart-wringing protest.

"I mean put it on right *now*," the Ranger said, "and stand against the back wall there."

Seeing no alternative—after all, he was staring into a gun barrel that looked as big as a tunnel—the salesman complied. The Ranger fired a single shot, which hit the vest just over the wearer's breastbone. Fortunately, the guarantee actually was valid, for the bullet never went through the steel plating, though it did knock the wind out of the salesman and left him with a horrendous bruise.

To avoid any hard feelings, the Ranger bought the vest and threw it into the nearest sump pit. The salesman left Borger the next day.

Joe Williams told me this story, a year or so after the event, when he and I were eating in the restaurant where he said it happened. (At that time Joe was promoting a new town site at Stinnett, a few miles north of Borger, and I drove him to both towns fairly often. To my disappointment, the country had quieted down considerably by that time.) Joe did not claim to be a witness, but said he heard about it from reliable friends who had been there. I think he believed it; I'm not sure whether I do or not.

Even ten Rangers were not enough to gentle down Borger. They had the cooperation of John A. Holmes, an honest and diligent young district attorney, who was prosecuting scores of criminal cases in spite of almost daily threats against his life. On

September 13, 1929, Holmes was shot down at his own door-step by an unidentified gunman hidden behind a vacant house next door. That was too much, even for a notoriously tolerant community. The resulting uproar led the governor to declare martial law before the month was out; he sent in enough troops to close the place up even tighter than the Rangers had, and from then on the oilmen could carry on their trade in relative tranquility.

Today Borger is a tidy little town, with a junior college, a concert association, and an earnest civic betterment movement. In 1969 it won an All American Cities award from the National Municipal League for its efforts to improve the quality of community life. But its population is less than half of what it was in its first year. My brother practiced law there for a while, but found it too quiet and moved on to Tulsa.

Frank Hamer was not the bravest man in the oil country. That title, by general acclamation, belonged to Tex Thornton. He was the specialist in blowing oil wells, a profession that had both an underground and a surface branch.

When a rig struck a modest vein of oil, the driller often thought he might increase the flow by setting off a heavy explosion at the bottom of the hole, to shatter the rock and thus speed up the seepage. In that case, he sent for Thornton. When Tex arrived at the drill site in his pickup truck, his first act was to order the crew and anybody else who happened to be around to move a least a mile away. Nobody ever objected. Then he began, very gently, to unload five gallon cans from his truck. From them he decanted, into smaller circular cans of a diameter that would fit comfortably into the drill hole, a yellowish, oily liquid. It was nitroglycerin, that powerful and highly sensitive explosive. Using long lines, Thornton would lower the circular cans one by one to the bottom of the hole, slowly and carefully so they would not bang against the casing en route.

When he had placed a charge he deemed adequate—perhaps
thirty gallons, perhaps more if the rock formation was particularly hard—Tex would drop a heavy wrench down the shaft
and quickly step back a few paces. The resulting mile-deep
explosion could sometimes be heard by the spectators, watching through binoculars from a mile away.

Occasionally, Tex would put on a little show for their benefit,
after the well blowing was finished. A microscopic film of nitroglycerin always remained on the inside of the empty five-gallon
cans. He would set them up, side by side, on the prairie and
then from a safe distance shoot a .22 bullet through the row of
cans. They disappeared with a spectacular flash, and enough
noise to satisfy an artilleryman.

The underground branch of Thornton's profession was tame
in comparison with his surface practice. The most delicate moment in drilling came immediately after the bit penetrated a
dome containing gas, or a mixture of gas and crude oil. As the
gas spewed out of the well head, with great force and an intimi-
dating roar, it might easily catch fire before the pipe could be
capped; a spark caused by rock fragments blowing out of the
hole and striking any piece of metal could be enough to set off
a giant torch. If the flow of gas was relatively small, men
dressed in asbestos suits and using long-handled tools just
might be able to shut off the flow. More often, the flame had to
be snuffed out—like a candle—by an explosion over the well
head. That was a job for Thornton and his crew of specialists.

One of their methods was to set up metal posts on opposite
sides of the well, one a few feet higher than the other and
perhaps two hundred yards apart. They would attach a cable to
the top of one post and then carry it in a semicircle around the
well to the other post, leaving the bight lying temporarily on
the ground. The loose end of the cable was passed through a
pulley on the top of the second post, so that at the strategic
moment it could be pulled taut to form a straight line running

a little to one side of the well head. Thornton planned the setup so that when he ordered the cable tightened, the part closest to the well would be only a foot or two above the ground. For that was a relatively cool zone; the gas had to rise a little distance before it could mix with enough oxygen to burn with maximum intensity. ("Relatively cool" in this case means something like "a suburb of hell.")

During that brief interval, Thornton and his helpers had to slide a trolley carrying a charge of explosive down the cable from the taller pole to the point nearest to the well head, and then set off the charge by means of a wire attached to its detonator. If everything went precisely right, the blast ought to blow out the flame.

But any number of things could go wrong. Before the shot, part of Thornton's crew would be playing streams of water on the well and its surroundings through high-pressure, long-range nozzles, in hopes of cooling off the pipe and drilling machinery so that hot metal would not reignite the fire. Consequently, the area would be so obscured with spray and clouds of steam that it was not easy to see the exact spot where the charge should be exploded. The cable might melt, or the trolley could jam, or the detonator might malfunction. Or, for unguessable reasons, the blast might fail to snuff out the flame—perhaps because the charge was too small, or the cable was not strung close enough. In that case the only thing to do was to start all over—maybe a half dozen times—until luck, skill, courage, and days of hard work in almost unbearable heat finally all meshed together. Once the fire was out, the well would simply be a hole in the ground, surrounded by scorched earth and twisted metal, spouting an invisible (but highly audible) column of gas. Then Thornton and his men could leave, and the roughnecks would begin the more prosaic job of capping the well.

Every moment of his working day, Thornton was in peril of

instant death. His truck was, of course, rigged with special safety equipment, including a complex set of rubber hammocks to cradle the nitro cans; even so, any unexpected bump as he drove over the prairie could have touched off his cargo. Handling the stuff was as touchy as handling a bushel of rattlesnakes.* Yet Tex never had a serious accident. He said it was simply a matter of knowing his job and taking it easy: "I never hurry, never get excited. I never make a move without thinking about it three times in advance." Some of his helpers had a different explanation. They insisted that his nervous system was strung with chilled copper wire.

In its early days the oil industry was spectacularly wasteful. Sometimes this was unavoidable. When a driller was exploring an unproven geological formation, he could not be expected to assemble storage tanks, much less lay a pipeline, on the off chance he might make a strike. When he did bring in a discovery well, then, the oil simply flowed onto the ground or into sump pits, until the shaft could be temporarily capped off aᵣ some arrangement made for shipment.

More waste, however, resulted from greed and ignorance. Often wells were drilled so close together that the derrick legs almost touched. From one to a dozen wells would have been enough to drain away all the oil and gas in that particular formation, at minimal cost. But lease brokers usually had subdivided the field into the smallest possible tracts, selling each of them to the highest bidder. Every leaseholder put down his well as fast as he could, and damn the expense, in hopes of getting as much oil as possible out of the pool before his rivals

---

* My consultant on explosives, Fred Olsen, for many years chief of research for Olin Corporation, tells me that safer chemicals were then well known—for example, trinitrotoluene, a dry, stable solid that cannot be set off by an ordinary shock or friction. But it was then reserved for military use. Mr. Olsen, incidentally, developed an advanced process for manufacturing smokeless powder that proved of crucial importance during World War II.

could reach it. A flagrant example was the Sour Lake field in southeast Texas, where Texaco made a big strike in 1903 on an 815-acre tract that it had leased. The company could have developed its own holdings in an orderly and economical fashion, if it had not been confronted with hundreds of independent operators who immediately began to drill just outside the boundaries of the Texaco land. Many derricks were set up on lots as small as twenty by twenty feet—barely enough room to operate the drilling equipment. Any of these wells that happened to tap the same geological stratum where Texaco had found oil could draw off thousands of barrels that otherwise would have gone to the discoverer. Consequently, Texaco had to drill more wells, and put them down more hastily, than it had originally intended; and the crowded condition of the neighboring operators resulted in many accidents, fires, and casualties among the roughnecks.

A gas well was often not considered to be worth the expense of capping. I have seen abandoned wells in the Texas Panhandle that vented millions of cubic feet of gas into the air for years on end, simply because nobody could think of anything to do with it, and the driller could not be bothered to shut off the flow. Around Borger in the thirties, much gas was burned to make carbon black, for use in tires, carbon paper, and other industrial products. Because the plants of that time used a woefully inefficient process, their chimneys spewed great billows of black smoke over the landscape day and night. When driving toward the town, you could see these dark plumes from twenty miles away.

As late as the forties gas retailed in Amarillo for about one cent per thousand cubic feet. To my parents, the cost of heating their house was the only expense that they considered negligible. Nobody in those days imagined such a thing as a fuel shortage. Most High Plains people really believed that their oil and gas supplies were inexhaustible, and fiercely resisted any

attempt at government regulation in the interests of conserva-
tion. They were, after all, spiritual descendants of the hide
hunters who had once believed that the buffalo herds would
last forever.

TWELVE

Unsettled Country

This fragmentary account of the settlement of the High Plains must remain unfinished, because in one important sense the country is still unsettled. It has not yet settled down to a stable state. Ever since the Alibates people quarried flint along the Canadian River fifteen centuries or more ago, the High Plains has gone through a series of turbulent and painful changes— and what may prove to be the most painful of all is now under way. The High Plains is running short of water.

The economic history of the country can best be understood as a series of mining ventures. The flint mines, which were the first, also lasted the longest. After they were abandoned, for reasons still uncertain, the High Plains remained virtually empty of people, until the Indians got horses from the Spaniards in the sixteenth century. Then they were able to mine the great buffalo herds that dominated the prairie. For about three hundred years, this Comanche-type economy was a stable one, because the Indians did not seriously deplete the herds; theirs was really a harvesting, rather than a mining operation. But when the white hide hunters arrived in 1873, the buffalo mining began in earnest, so this natural resource was exhausted within a decade.

The cattlemen who followed the hunters in effect mined grass. Overgrazing was common during the first big cattle boom, and was one of the factors—along with drought and unprecedented blizzards—that led to the boom's collapse in the 1880s. It was by no means universal. The better ranchers, from Colonel Goodnight to Lee Bivins and Tom Britt, were always careful not to graze more cattle than the land could sustain—often no more than one animal to thirty acres. But the greedier cowmen overstocked their land until the dust and sandstorms of the early thirties taught them a harsh, and sometimes final, lesson.*

Overgrazing is unusual on the High Plains today. But in the years from World War I till the mid-thirties another malpractice turned out to be even more destructive—the mining of the soil by wheat farmers. In that period, these farmers plowed up hundreds of thousands of acres of good pasture land for a purpose God never intended. In much of that country the rainfall is too scant and erratic, and the earth too vulnerable to wind erosion, to make wheat raising without irrigation a dependable enterprise. Again, the dust storms of the thirties blew this lesson into a lot of stubborn heads. Since then, many one-time wheat fields—including some where I once drove a tractor—have gone back to grass, and most of the remaining wheat land is at least partially protected from erosion by contour plowing

---

* (In 1932 I drove a Model T Ford from Oklahoma City to Amarillo while a Blue Norther was blowing—a steady fifty-mile wind sweeping down from the North Pole over hundreds of miles of prairie denuded by drought and bad land management. I had to wear a wet handkerchief tied around my face to keep from choking; and by the time I reached Amarillo, the right or north side of the car was scoured down to bright metal as if it had been sand blasted—as in fact, it had. An incalculable tonnage of topsoil blew away on that day alone.

and other improved tillage practices. But in the meantime, a lot of land was sorely damaged.

The oil and gas boom was, of course, a pure mining venture from the start, and a highly profitable one. Some of the old wells are still pumping oil, or flowing a much diminished stream of natural gas. Yet, inevitably, their output diminishes from year to year, and the exploratory drilling has virtually stopped. Small "oil patches" may still be found someday on the High Plains, but the discovery of another major field is most unlikely. The petroleum geologists have already scrutinized every acre pretty thoroughly.

The sixth mining venture on the High Plains, and probably the last, was for water. When my parents homesteaded their land, they got a modest amount of water—enough for household use and their livestock—from shallow wells pumped by windmills or from the rare sweet-water streams such as Dozier Creek. This was water replenished every year by rainfall. (Well, almost every year. In a prolonged drought, some of the wells went dry and the streams disappeared.) After a succession of such dry years, my kinfolks, the Britts, put dams across every gully and arroyo on their ranch near Shamrock, swearing that if it ever did rain again, not a drop would escape from their property. The resulting ponds have been a blessing, not only to the Britts and their cattle, but to visitors like me who have fished them for bass.

In 1911 a farmer in Hale County discovered a new source of water, not dependent on replenishment from the clouds. He drilled a deep well into what he thought was an underground river, bringing an everlasting supply of water down from the Rocky Mountains. We now know that he had tapped a geological formation known as the Ogallala Aquifer, a lens-shaped bed of gravel up to three hundred feet thick that extends from Nebraska to North Texas. For millions of years it had been accumulating water, like a giant underground reservoir—some of it possibly from surface seepage, most of it probably from an era when the climate of the Great Plains was a good deal wetter.

Until World War II, this buried treasure was not used for irrigation on a large scale, primarily because the stratum lay too deep in most places to be pumped with wind power. The discovery of abundant natural gas solved that problem; an old automobile engine, adapted to burn gas, can bring up five hundred gallons a minute from a depth of two hundred feet or more. Even so, as late as 1948 only about a million acres of Texas Panhandle land was under irrigation. Today the total runs above 6 million acres, making the High Plains the largest irrigated area on the continent aside from the Central Valley of California. Its ditches are being fed from more than seventy thousand wells.

The coming of irrigation changed the character of life on the High Plains as drastically as the discovery of oil had done a generation earlier. For it is an economic fact of life that most Americans do not like beef from cattle fed on grass alone. (I do. To me, it tastes better than grain-fed beef—but I admit that it is tougher, and has less of the cholesterol that my friends find so delicious.) Because of this almost universal preference for fat beef, the High Plains ranchers had traditionally shipped their steers east for a final fattening in the feed lots of Illinois and Iowa (which raise an abundance of corn) and then for slaughter in the packing houses of Chicago and other Midwestern cities. When water from the Ogallala Aquifer began to flow in torrents, this was no longer necessary. For the first time, local farmers could raise enough feed grains—mostly milo maize and sorghums—to "top off" all the cattle raised in the Texas and Oklahoma Panhandles. That meant a lot more money for the ranchers, who no longer had to freight their cattle East, and who could now put on at home the extra poundage that earlier had proved so profitable to the feed lot owners in Illinois.

By 1970 so many feed lots had been built in the Texas Panhandle that they could handle a million cattle at a time—which means about 3 million a year, since the beasts stand at the grain troughs for only three months before reaching optimum weight. Along with the feed lots came slaughter and packing plants, many of them designed to produce, not chilled carcasses in the traditional fashion, but boxed beef. As a result, industrial employment in and around Amarillo reached an all-time high in the mid-seventies, and the entire High Plains were more prosperous than I had ever seen them. For the first time, all of my known kinfolk were living in modest comfort and a few of them were well off.

This bright picture contains only one dark streak. The whole complex of cattle feeding and beef packing depends on the Ogallala Aquifer—and that reservoir is being mined fairly fast. The rate of depletion varies considerably from place to place, but in general the underground water supply is running out most rapidly in the lower part of the Texas Panhandle, where the gravel bed containing it is thinnest. South of Lubbock, wells that used to pump a thousand gallons a minute are now dry and abandoned. Further north the situation is not yet so serious. One closely observed well on an agricultural experiment station west of Amarillo used to produce eight hundred gallons per minute in 1960; by 1976 it was still flowing five hundred gallons. Yet the water level throughout the whole region continues to fall inexorably—on some farms only a few inches a year, on others as much as seven feet. The most plausible estimates I have been able to get suggest that about half of the water that the Ogallala formation originally held was exhausted by 1977, and that virtually all of the rest will be gone within thirty or forty years. Meanwhile, the cost of fuel for pumping it is becoming almost prohibitive.

This is not a popular subject on the High Plains. For as long as I can remember, anybody who brought up the question of water depletion was regarded as at best rude, and at worst a traitor to his neighbors. Chamber of Commerce officials and land speculators have always been particularly touchy. Anson R. Bertrand, dean of the College of Agricultural Sciences at Texas Technological University in Lubbock, was recently quoted by the *New York Times* as saying: "One thing that has appalled me is the head-in-the-sand attitude taken by people in this area. They don't want to face the issue that water is on the way out. . . ." And one of his colleagues, James E. Osborn, chairman of the university's agricultural economics department, added that, when he first came to the High Plains in 1965, "I couldn't go to a farm meeting and talk about it. It was like talking to a room full of people who wouldn't listen. I've been told by some people to keep it to myself and to shut up."*

But some people are talking about it now. When a Texas politician brings up the subject, it is nearly always by way of introduction to some visionary scheme for bringing in water to recharge the aquifer, by ditch or pipeline from Canada or the Mississippi River. Lyndon B. Johnson used to talk with exceptional eloquence about such possibilities, at least in the days before he became President. When he sat in the White House and had to think of the billions that such projects would cost, he spoke of them less often. Nonpolitical Texans have seldom taken such talk seriously. They know that Canada is not about to sell its water to the High Plains, and that even if the money could be found to import water from there or from the Mississippi—most unlikely, in view of the chronic federal deficit—the engineering problems would be enormous, if not insuperable.

A few sober-minded people are looking for more practical solutions, or at least ways to postpone the inevitable. The research station near Amarillo, run jointly by the United States Department of Agriculture and Texas A. and M. University, is seeking to develop crops that are less thirsty. The station's director, B. A. Stewart, says that: "A maximum yield isn't the

---

New York Times, March 21, 1977, in an article by James P. Sterba.

objective any longer. We are trying to get a maximum trade, pounds of wheat for gallons of water. If all the water goes, production will drop sixty percent in the Panhandle."

He realizes, of course, that it is not really a question of "if" but of "when"—and millions of people outside the High Plains should wish him well in his efforts to put off the Dry-up Day as long as possible. When it finally arrives, a lot of them will have to find their bread grain somewhere else, and others will have to learn to eat grass-fed beef.

The possibility of such a future for the High Plains had never occurred to me when I left them—temporarily, I then thought—in 1933. Since my graduation from the University of Oklahoma a little more than a year earlier, I had been working as a reporter on the *Daily Oklahoman* in Oklahoma City, under the tutelage of an extraordinary editor, Walter Harrison. Unlike most newspaper executives of that time, he believed it important for all his reporters to learn to write as well as their talents, however meager, could be stretched. To that end, he slaved over our copy, weeding out adjectives, cursing our clichés, praising an occasional apt phrase, and often demanding one rewrite after another. Sometimes we hated him for it, but most of us learned something. Many of the youngsters he trained in the early thirties went on to better jobs—among them were top executives of both the Gannett and the Knight newspaper chains, a White House correspondent for the Associated Press, a leading foreign correspondent for the *New York Times,* several successful novelists, and editors of a dozen newspapers and magazines.

One spring day in 1933, Harrison left a note on my desk suggesting that I try to write a feature story about a fortune teller who was offering her services to the patrons of a local nightclub. She turned out to be a scrawny, middle-aged woman dressed in a sleazy gypsy costume and equipped with a crystal ball. At the beginning of our interview, she apologized for these props. The management insisted on them, she said, "to give the act a little class." She added that she never actually saw anything in the crystal ball, and had never before attempted any commercial fortune telling. Her name was Mrs. Mamie Grimes. A couple of weeks earlier she and her husband had lost their farm through foreclosure of the mortgage—like thousands of other Oklahomans who were ruined by the Dust Bowl and the Great Depression. In desperation, she had applied for the fortune-telling job, because she had been gifted from childhood with what she called "second sight." That is, she could sometimes talk to a person for a little while, preferably while touching his hand or arm, and pictures might come into her head about what was going to happen to him in the future. This was an intermittent gift, she explained; often no pictures came, and when they did they were sometimes meaningless. But since it was the only talent she had, aside from farming, she had persuaded the nightclub manager to let her try her luck in return for whatever tips she could pick up. Would I like to see what she could do in my case?

I was of course as cynical as any proper young reporter, but her candor struck me as both pathetic and touching, so I agreed. She pushed the ball aside, laid a callused hand on my wrist, and closed her eyes.

A few minutes later she said, "I think I see something. A blue airplane. Are you planning a plane trip?"

No.

"Well," she went on, "I see a ship too—a ship with two smoke stacks. And I see the dome of a big building, something like the photos of the Capitol in Washington. And a lot of little flags. And I think I see a column of words, or rather the same word repeated several times. I can't quite make it out. 'Copyright,' maybe. What does 'copyright' mean?"

I said it didn't mean anything to me, since the items I wrote for the paper were never copyrighted.

She said she couldn't see any more pictures, and apologized

because those that had drifted through her head didn't seem to add up to anything significant. I tipped her one dollar—the most my expense account was good for—and went back to the office to write a sentimental little story about the odd fate that could befall an Oklahoma farm woman in the depths of the depression. The copy desk cut it to a couple of paragraphs.

A week later I had a phone call from Joe Brandt, who had been one of my favorite teachers at the University. He suggested that I apply for a Rhodes scholarship; Oklahoma didn't seem to have many likely candidates that year, and I was still eligible even though I was no longer an undergraduate. Mostly to humor him, I did apply. The faculty members who interviewed me, all former Rhodes scholars, decided—to my astonishment—to send me on to the regional selection committee that would meet a few days later in New Orleans. Walter Harrison gave me two days leave and Bennie Turner, our aviation reporter, arranged a pass for the trip on Braniff Airlines.

When I got to the airport, I found that the DC-2 Braniff usually flew on that route was laid up for repairs. The airline—then a small local outfit—had no standby equipment, so it had hired a substitute from a charter service—a small single-engine blue plane. The coincidence struck me as curious, and I made a mental note to tell Mrs. Grimes about it when I got back.

By happy accident, one member of the New Orleans selection committee was Edgar Stern, editor of the *Times-Picayune*. He seemed interested in me, because no working newspaperman had ever appeared before the committee; and during the two-hour interview he steered the questioning toward subjects about which he presumed I might know something. I was grateful, but I still did not take the proceedings very seriously because I regarded myself—then as now—as a reporter rather than a scholar, and considered that I had practically no chance against the eleven other candidates. In our waiting room conversations, they had all seemed awesomely more learned than I could ever be.

It was Stern, I suspect, who eventually swung the committee's vote in my favor. When the examiners announced their decision late that night, I was one of the scholars they had chosen. The other was David St. Clair, also an Oklahoman, who had worked his way through the university by serving as night guard at an insane asylum; eventually he became a metallurgical geologist of international distinction, discovering major deposits of iron, copper, and other metals on four continents. Both of us were too surprised to say anything beyond a few dazed words of thanks. Then we went out to find a speakeasy on Rampart Street and ordered the fanciest drinks we had ever heard of—pousse-cafés. (I have never been tempted to try another.)

A few months later David and I sailed for England with thirty-four other newly chosen Rhodes scholars aboard the Dutch steamer *Veendam*. It had two funnels. Again, I noted the coincidence and regretted that I had forgotten to tell Mrs. Grimes about the blue airplane.

At the time I had every intention of returning to Oklahoma City or Amarillo after three years of studying politics, philosophy, and economics at Oxford. Someday, I hoped, I might become editor of a paper on the High Plains, as my father had been; the country suited me. But luck decided otherwise; other temptations intervened.

Still, during all the decades since 1933 I have returned to the High Plains on frequent visits, because my family lived there and because, even now, I get bouts of homesickness for that harsh and unforgettable landscape. A small-boat sailor finds it hard to explain why he returns again and again to the sea, in spite of all the cold wet nights, the fogs, the dismaying storms, and the multitude of other discomforts he has suffered. So it is with the High Plains. For one who grows up there, the endless horizons, the heat, the wind, the spectacular electrical storms, the Blue Northers of winter, the easily found solitude, and the very spareness of life become nostalgic memories.

Within their lifetimes, I expect my children to see the High

Plains revert to something not very different from what it was when I left it. The water from the Ogallala Aquifer will be gone, and so will the oil and gas, or they will remain only in token amounts, like the buffalo. The feed lots and the packing plants may be gone too, or they could keep going for a while on grain imported from somewhere else. Some cattle may again be shipped East for fattening. But it is more likely that the skyrocketing increase in the world's population will, in thirty or forty years, make grain too precious to feed to livestock. What beef is packed around Amarillo will probably be lean and grass fed. And it may well come from Beefalo, rather than Herefords and Black Angus.

Then the landscape will be dominated once more by grazing animals, as it was in Colonel Goodnight's day. Some grains and cotton will still be dry farmed, as they were in my boyhood, but the acreage will be much reduced, and much less lucrative than it is now. For the rule of thumb is that without irrigation Panhandle land will produce good crops about a third of the time, barely harvestable crops another third, and nothing at all in the other years.

Conceivably the High Plains will find new industries to replace those based on gas and oil and irrigation—but it is hard to guess what they might be, since little else exists in the way of natural resources except grass. My hunch is that it could someday produce a considerable amount of electric power from giant windmills and solar heat collectors. Wind and sunshine are assets the country has in plenty.

Not all of us old Texans are persuaded that the change will be entirely tragic. The population of the High Plains may dwindle, and millionaires and Cadillacs will not be so thick on the ground. For most ordinary people, life there probably will be leaner and harder, as it was for Joe Williams on the RO ranch and the Capertons on the Salt Fork and the Fischers at Texhoma. But never mind. The old-timers got along somehow, and a lot of them were just as happy as if they had owned Cadillacs. I suspect their descendants will make out just as well.

Acknowledgments

I owe a special debt of gratitude to four historians of the Old West: Edward Everett Dale and Carl Coke Rister, who were my teachers at the University of Oklahoma, 1928–32; and Frank Dobie and Walter Prescott Webb, both of the University of Texas, who were my friends in later years. They all stimulated my interest in the High Plains, and their books are among the most cherished in my library. Since this does not pretend to be an academic history, there is no point in my listing the many other books and articles I have consulted, though some of the more interesting ones are mentioned in the text. Readers who want to explore further into Western history will have no trouble in finding plenty of good bibliographies. For example, an excellent one is included in Frederick W. Rathjen's *The Texas Panhandle Frontier* (Austin: University of Texas Press, 1973). Perhaps, however, I should mention a publication little known even among historians—*Sturm's Oklahoma Magazine,* published for about a decade in Oklahoma City early in this century; it printed many accounts of the early settlement of the state that are not available elsewhere.

Much of the material in this book came from family papers and the recollection of relatives, most of them now dead. Among those who survive, I am especially indebted to: Charles and Polly SoRelle and Miriam Caperton of Amarillo, Texas, who have supplied me not only with documents but with food, lodging, and transportation during my research in the High Plains; Helen Barkley of Shamrock, Texas; and Mrs. Paul Laune of Phoenix, Arizona.

My mother always believed that she was of Scotch-Irish descent. However, when Bernard M. Caperton published his genealogical volume, *The Caperton Family*, (Charlottesville, Va., 1973) he concluded that "it is most probable that the Capertons were French Huguenots who sojourned in England for a time before coming to America. . . ." John Caperton, who migrated to Virginia sometime before 1753, occasionally spelled his name "Capebritton." He married a Scottish woman, Polly Thompson, and all of the numerous Capertons now living in this country are believed to be their descendants.

The illustrator of this book, the late Paul Laune of Phoenix, Arizona, grew up in Woodward, Oklahoma, and studied art in Chicago, New York, and Rome. He became one of the best known of Western artists, specializing in landscapes, portraits, and book illustrations. One of his last major works was a series of six murals, depicting the early history of Oklahoma and the High Plains, in the Woodward Pioneer Museum.

ABOUT THE AUTHOR

JOHN FISCHER is an associate editor of *Harper's Magazine*, where he was editor in chief from 1953 to 1968. Before that time he was an editor of general books for Harper & Brothers, a European correspondent for United Press, and a Washington reporter with Associated Press. A graduate of the University of Oklahoma, he also attended Oxford University as a Rhodes Scholar. He is the author of four earlier books and many magazine articles, mainly on public affairs.